PSYCHOLOG(
POWER OF M̶L̶_̶_̶_̶_̶_̶
THE FORMULA FOR VICTORY

Psychological Warfare is a psychological self-help book that explores the crisis mindset and teaches the reader to identify previous patterns of negative behavior, practice small yet actionable changes, and be proactive in future moments of conflict. Psychological Warfare posits that the power to influence the outcomes of any confrontation rests on making small, easy changes to one's own behavior, an empowering message of strength in the face of adversity. The book includes various personal anecdotes from the author's life to illustrate particular psychological tenets, with action-item lists and suggestions for reflection punctuating each chapter. It maintains a conversational, occasionally-irreverent tone, and seamlessly blends scientific-based research, personal narrative, and insightful advice.

"Poppi effectively and clearly explains the tools and strategies she's developed over the last 20 years. If you're just starting out in your career or are looking to get ahead in the corporate world, this book is definitely worth a read."—*Natalie Cochran, Design Studio Owner*

"Poppi has written a book that challenges you to empower yourself and not fall victim to life circumstances that might otherwise cripple you. With relatable and raw honesty (and a good dose of humor), she provides effective strategies and powerful tools to navigate through difficult professional and personal situations. This book is for everyone who seeks to build inner confidence, and for those who no longer want moments of intense emotional experiences to dictate their behavior and destiny."—*Jaime Cohen, Ph.D.*

"I've NEVER read a self-help book in my life. I read this one cover to cover."—*Mike Morrison, Energy Trader*

"Poppi's book is the perfect blueprint for surviving and thriving in the 21st century. I wish I had access to this when I first started out in my adult life, professionally and personally. The wisdom she's gained from her trial and error experiences are generously shared with us with both her painful honesty and tremendous wit. Wit being key to keeping me reading anything. You have to love someone that can go from king fu wisdom to accidental boob postings and not lose the message!"—*Colleen Stelmaszek, Executive Assistant*

PSYCHOLOGICAL WARFARE
The Power of Mental Strength and the
Formula for Victory

Poppi Z

Moonshine Cove Publishing, LLC
Abbeville, South Carolina U.S.A.
First Moonshine Cove edition November 2018

ISBN: 978-1-945181-481
Library of Congress PCN: 2018962280
Copyright 2018 by Poppi Z Melera

Book cover design by Nick Courtright at Atmosphere Press

About the Author

Poppi Z's background is geographically varied, professionally diverse, and filled with moments of both crisis and conviction—factors all leading to the creation of her entertaining and energizing self-help manual *Psychological Warfare: The Power of Mental Strength and the Formula for Victory*. With nearly two decades of corporate experience under her belt, Poppi turned her attention to aggregating the lessons she learned into an engaging, accessible manual, whose message is one of empowerment, humor, and positive and proactive change.

Poppi is the founder and managing partner of The Z Firm, an oil and gas recruiting and staffing firm that specializes in the permanent placement of professionals in various sectors of the energy business. Prior to founding her own business, Poppi worked in energy operations spanning multiple commodities including natural gas, power, coal, and petroleum products. As a result, she has a strong understanding of the nuances of corporate culture, as well as significant psychological insight into conflict management and resolution, and often draws on these strengths in her writing.

Recently, Poppi has launched the nonprofit organization Scoutz, an organization committed to empowering college graduates who are entering the workforce by providing experienced professional mentors to assist with career advice, resume writing, interviewing skills, professional attire, corporate nuances and much more.

Poppi holds a Bachelor of Science in Psychology and a minor in Marketing from the University of Houston. Currently, she is an active supporter of several professional organizations and charities serving women in business, military and veterans, and youth advocacy. Together, she and her husband, John, have six beautiful children. *Psychological Warfare* is her first book.

Http://www.poppiz-us.com

PSYCHOLOGICAL WARFARE

Preface

Have you ever let your emotions get the best of you to the point where you lost the ability to think logically or rationally? Within the pages of *Psychological Warfare,* you will read edifying personal stories on how to sift through intense moments and take notice of the destructive habits and pieces of information that cause our brains to short-circuit. You will learn a strategy and a set of behaviors you can apply in both personal and professional situations. By training your mind to function rationally under pressure, you acquire the ability to operate from the driver's seat even when you find yourself in the back seat. When you find yourself in a heated argument, when you have a difficult choice to make, or even when you are simply dealing with stress and anxiety, the tools I am about to show you will help you succeed and live your best life.

*Psychological Warfa*re is a book about keeping a strong mind during a crisis, and it discusses the tools needed to navigate through tough situations with dignity and finesse. Arming oneself with specific psychological strategies can turn a losing situation into a winning one.

In business and in my personal life, I have often found myself sitting across from a client or ex-spouse, negotiating myself right into a hole. By falling prey to criticism and false allegations, by lacking confidence, by reacting out of anger, by not being prepared, or by surrendering out of fear, I did not get a favorable outcome. However, through a challenging process of trial and error, I learned a game-changing method for turning the tables and gaining advantage over my opponent. I did this by using a defined set of psychological tools. In times of stress, fear, or venturing into the unknown, these tools empowered me to negotiate from a place of strength and unlocked the secret to achieving a commendable outcome. I became more confident and was able to conduct myself in a way that led me to achieve the goals I had set out for myself. These are the tools I will teach you how to use in *Psychological Warfare*.

Whether you are confronting problems in your personal or professional affairs, facing legal issues, navigating a divorce, coping with a death in the family, asking for a raise, dealing with a horrible boss, deceptive coworker, or disgruntled employee — in fact, whenever you are working through any psychologically challenging issue — you must have a plan. You must have a set of tools and a map to maneuver through each challenge successfully. *Psychological Warfare* is the secret weapon everyone needs to play the game called LIFE.

Before I dive into the impactful knowledge that will guide you to a victorious outcome, I would like to tell you a little bit about myself. My professional background is in the energy industry. From 1995 to 2006, prior to founding my own business, I worked in energy operations roles primarily focused around the environment of the trading floor and spanning multiple energy commodities including natural gas, power, coal, and petroleum products. Having supported trading and marketing from both middle-office risk and operations to back-office accounting, I have a strong understanding of trade floor environments, corporate structures, and related processes. My operational expertise comes from working with a variety of companies, including merchant energy, investment banks, and pipelines in Houston and Connecticut. As a result, I have excellent knowledge of the nuances of corporate culture, specifically as it relates to the energy business.

In 2006, I was scouted out and introduced to the recruiting industry, where I held expanding leadership roles within the energy recruiting sector as a director of commodities search. I developed and managed significant client relationships and led recruitment efforts focused on professionals in trading, risk management, accounting, compliance, and IT for the energy industry.

I am the founder and president of Scoutz, a not-for-profit organization committed to empowering college graduates who are entering the workforce by providing experienced professional mentors to assist with career advice, résumé writing, interviewing skills, professional attire, corporate nuances, and much more. Scoutz aims to build confidence and turns rookie graduates into rock-star employees.

I hold a Bachelor of Science degree in Psychology, with a minor in Marketing, from the University of Houston. I am an active supporter of several professional organizations and charities, including National Energy Services Association, Young Professionals in Energy, Texas Women in Business, Wounded Warriors (supporting military and veterans), Avondale House (supporting people with autism), Night Court (Houston's all-lawyer charity), Grassroots Soccer (focused on eliminating the adolescent health gap), Houston Performing Arts, Toys for Tots (providing toys and gifts for less-fortunate children), and the Malala Fund (championing girls' rights). Together, my husband, John, and I have six beautiful children: each of us has two boys and a girl from previous marriages.

In 2012, while deciding whether to accept a partnership at a recruiting firm or start my own firm, I found myself lacking a clear vision of what I wanted to achieve. Struggling with feelings of loyalty and fear of the unknown, I created, through trial and error, a method to guide me to a positive outcome. One way or another, a choice had to be made — should I stay or should I go? By using a few simple psychological tools, I could break the problem down into smaller, more manageable pieces, get control over my anxiety, and feel confident in the choice I made. There was no right or wrong choice, only peace of mind after the choice was made. My choice was to start The Z Firm Energy Recruiting in Houston, Texas. The tools I developed to help me make my decision eventually became the basis of *Psychological Warfare*.

Chapter 1
Perceiving Leads to Believing

Why is it that some people can walk into a room and command attention immediately, radiating confidence and floating through a crowd with seamless grace? Picture it: someone impeccably dressed, confident, and intelligent; someone who might be surrounded by the cream of society — Ivy League educations, successful careers, prominent family names, tremendous wealth, summer homes in the Hamptons, cottages in France, private planes at their fingertips. This is the world of the extremely wealthy, arrogant, and egocentric personality types, yet our fearless individual can ingratiate themselves among them, talk their talk, walk their walk, and act like they own the place. They appear to be untouchable, unscathed by negativity, and void of any feeling of insecurity. They exude an air of self-confidence, but all the while they cannot hold a candle to the elite in terms of education, pedigree, or finances. In fact, this particular individual I want to tell you about had no college degree, no wealth, no famous ancestors, and no significant accomplishments to speak of.

In the summer of 2000, when I was twenty-five, I got married and drove roughly 1,700 miles, from Houston, Texas, to Stamford, Connecticut, with a dog and a U-Haul in one weekend. Within two weeks I had landed a job as a derivatives analyst at an investment bank located in Greenwich, Connecticut.

The investment bank sat along the Hudson River, with its breathtaking sunsets and fantastic views. To say it was beautiful is an understatement; it was extraordinary. The company employed the largest number of wealthy professionals I had ever seen in one office. I wasn't sure why they would be interested in hiring me — there was nothing Ivy League in my background, but I did have some good bullshit!

When I initially interviewed for the position at the investment bank, the Human Resources representative asked me if I had a thick skin. I smiled and told him, "Yes, I am a middle child." He chuckled and asked me if I had brothers. I said, "No, I have three sisters, and they will psychologically gut you if they don't get what they want; brothers would have been a cakewalk." I was exaggerating slightly; however, he must have liked my answer, because he offered me the job. I learned then that sometimes confidence matters more than background.

Walking on the trade floor for the first time was extremely intimidating. There were about 100 to 150 people working on the floor; the male to female ratio was about nine to one, and very few women held high-level positions. My job was a junior-level analyst. My supervisor escorted me around the floor, introducing me to the different executive groups and explaining how the trade floor was structured. Televisions were mounted throughout the trade floor, displaying multiple news stations, and a stock market ticker ran across the bottom of each screen. Busy phone lines rang constantly, and there were rows and rows of small cubicles with desks filled with papers and computer screens that displayed graphs, charts, emails, and stock market information. The trade floor was so busy and intoxicating, with the hustle and bustle of a hive and people fluidly moving around each other like worker bees with incredible urgency. As I walked aisle by aisle, being introduced to traders and analysts, I shook hands and smiled ear to ear with nervous energy. I said hello to anyone who passed by me, even if they didn't return the greeting or even acknowledge me. The lack of friendliness made me a bit uneasy. Being raised in the South, I was taught to be warm and friendly to everyone, and it was the only way I knew how to communicate. But this world was different. This was the business world; people are unwelcoming, and they are unapologetic about it. Although I was a fish out of water, I liked it. The atmosphere was intense and finding my footing in this new environment was invigorating.

The cast of characters on the trade floor was somewhat stereotypical of what I perceived Wall Street to be like, and it provided me with great mental stimulation. I found myself people watching throughout the day; there was so much great material to indulge my curiosity that it became my favorite pastime. As I studied the men, I noticed that they were very observant of each other, but they were even more observant of the attractive women, mostly administrative assistants and analysts, who passed by their desks. They were also an interesting breed of storytellers, always bragging about their escapades from the night before, or the smoking-hot new Porsche they had just purchased, or how smart they were because they'd graduated from Stanford.

On their desks stood pictures of their wives and children, along with a copy of the most recent *Wall Street Journal,* crossword puzzles, and various reports. One trader had on his desk an actual wooden chess set with all the little pieces. It was intense to see him jump out of his seat and scream at another trader and then sit back down and make a move on his chessboard. I wondered how the traders were able to maintain focus in the stressful environment of a trade floor and play a game of strategy like chess, but they did. It became clear that operating under pressure was a must in this environment, or you would be eaten alive.

Most of the women on the trade floor, whether admins, analysts or traders, were attractive; they were thin, with long dark hair and minimal makeup. They carried themselves with an air of self-importance and superiority. A new female colleague, especially an attractive one, was perceived as a threat and therefore was not welcomed easily — she had to earn her way into the group. I spent the first six months playing up to egos in an effort to disarm the women and try to make allies. They enjoyed boasting about their superior social lives and spoke freely about going to the Hamptons for the weekend, which is where the truly wealthy have vacation homes and go out to socialize. I was not familiar with the whole East Coast world, so it was something I had to learn. One of my coworkers who sat next to me quickly inserted herself into a conversation to let me know that she was having an affair with one of the married traders, whom she spent time with at his house in the "Hamps." My eyes got big and my mouth opened slightly. I was a little surprised at her admission of the affair, and that she seemed so pleased with herself, as if she had impressed me. I knew at that very moment I was not to go near that trader — she was marking her territory. I was newly married and had no interest in being involved in such a mess. I simply noted her warning to stay away and went about my business.

One of the more senior girls who worked in my group (I will call her "K" because "bitch" takes too long to type) went out of her way to show me she was the boss and to impress upon me how things were going to work. She took every opportunity to remind me that her position in the company was far above mine, and that I was to know my place. After every interaction, I was less and less impressed with her attitude. What was the point of being that hostile?

K was in her late twenties, with shoulder-length jet-black hair, pale white skin, and a perfect petite figure to die for. She looked a lot like Monica from *Friends*, only her personality was not neurotic or funny, just calculating and unpleasant. K carried herself in a smooth, uppity shrew manner and exuded the confidence of a lion. Although she was not my supervisor, she enjoyed taking advantage of my "new-girl–ness" by being domineering and imperious, as if I were a lowly grunt. K especially enjoyed instructing me to do subservient tasks in front of the senior executives, like "Get me three copies of today's numbers and go ahead and order lunch for the other analysts and yourself." My observation of K was that she had a perceived superiority over others, mainly women in her professional surroundings. There were consequences for those who dared to threaten her social order, and she would quickly have them cast out. It wasn't until months later that I realized that all women posed a threat to K.

The senior executives loved K, and the buzz around the office was that she had the potential to become a successful trader. My direct supervisor, who happened to be a woman, confided in me that the senior executives were going to sponsor K to get her Series 3 brokerage license. This was a big deal because it not only cost the company a few hundred dollars for the prep classes and test fees, it showed that they were investing in someone and their potential to move into a trading role. K had been with the company for a few years, so she had more tenure than I did, but not more overall work experience. A six-week training course and hundreds of dollars later, K claimed to be sick and didn't show up the day of the test. I'm not sure if this surprised others on the trade floor; however, it did not surprise me. There was something about K I just wasn't buying. She had already proven to be manipulative and demeaning, so when she happened to fall ill on the very day of the test, I knew there was an episode of trickery up her sleeve. K was stalling and trying to drag the process out until she could figure out her next move. Naturally, she rescheduled the test for another date and ended up canceling the test for a second time. The third time, K finally showed up and took the test. She didn't pass. In fact, per my supervisor, who received K's score, she failed the test miserably. Interestingly enough, my supervisor did not care for K either and was not surprised by her actions. Although she didn't directly say she did not like K, I could tell by the sly smile that sprawled across her face when she confided in me about K's failures.

K took her deceitful behavior as far as she could, but in the end, she was exposed for everything she was trying desperately to hide, and her shenanigans stopped working. The same coworker who had previously told me about her affair with the trader and the house in the "Hamps" spilled the beans about K having an affair with another one of the married traders. When K was told she would not be moving into a trading role — unsurprising, because she had not passed the securities test — she played the only card she had left, which was sexual harassment and extortion. And there was no way K was going to show defeat — she had to save face at all cost. K went straight to HR and revealed every detail about the torrid affair and made claims of sexual harassment. Fortunately for the trader she was having an affair with, he made millions of dollars for the company, so he was considered very valuable; however, K didn't hold the same value. The company had invested time and money in K, and she hadn't performed as expected. Who knows why K didn't pass the test — perhaps she wasn't as smart as everyone thought, or perhaps she wasn't qualified in the first place but just appeared overly confident. Personally, I think K was waiting for a shortcut on the test, a way to cheat, but she couldn't find a way to make it happen. She knew nothing about securities, commodities, or trading and wasn't very good with numbers, so it would have been an outlier had she passed, more like a miracle. Regardless of the reasons, the fact remained that she didn't make the cut in the end.

Although K had no prior performance issues, she had gained a reputation for being difficult to deal with, and now for being manipulative and cunning. Previously, exceptions had been made for K from upper management because she was perceived as much brighter than she was and was thought to have greater potential than she had. However, by not passing the test she lost respect instantly, and the game was over. The company offered K a financial settlement to make her go away. I have no idea what the figure was, but it must have been good, because she took the money and ran. Although her allegations probably held some truth, it was largely a convoluted mess of lies. K was not a victim of horrible injustice; she was simply a fraud. And probably a psychopath.

K's exit from the company was an event that seemed unthinkable. She unleashed a Human Resources nightmare that the executives tried desperately to contain through silence. My supervisor pulled me aside, with a slight grin on her face, and informed me that K would not be coming back. After that, nobody spoke about why K was no longer with the company or where she was going. She had simply moved on.

The one tool K had mastered over all others was her ability to maintain mental control in intimidating situations. She had a high school education, mediocre professional experience, a fearless attitude, and confidence to push forward. However, the perceived advantages K had over others were simply a placebo effect. She was beautiful and appeared competent on the outside, but she was riddled with insecurity and apprehension on the inside. K's biggest fear was that people would figure out she wasn't that smart, that she wasn't qualified to be a trader-in-training, that she wasn't educated, that her competence wasn't near what people thought it was, and that she wasn't as sagacious as she pretended to be. K was a giant fraud and she knew it, so she went to great lengths to find fault with and demean others to make herself appear and feel superior. And it worked, for a short period of time; but in the end the mask came off and the true K was exposed.

Even though K was in a situation that presented her with a great difficulty, she wasn't fazed. She psychologically deflected her opponents to the point where they were not able to hone in on her deceit. The executives had formed an opinion of K's abilities by largely ignoring her behavior and rewarding her by giving her advantages. The preferential treatment she was getting probably also had something to do with the trader she was sleeping with. He must have put in a good word on her behalf with management.

K's greatest affliction was her lack of self-esteem. I should have looked at the situation differently when she acted demeaning and spoke to me in sharp tones. I had to work with her and couldn't avoid her entirely. But, had I understood that K was largely insecure and felt threatened, which is why she treated people as if they were below her status, I could have emotionally defused her. Instead, I gave her way too much power. I needed a better technique and some perspective.

Learning to detect such individuals is an important tool to use in protecting yourself from unnecessary complexity, conflict, and immense stress. While their physical appearance and their intellectual abilities will vary, you will know them by their behavior. Toxic individuals skew your reality with their false sense of confidence, which is simply a state of mind but not a measure of authenticity. They aim to hinder your growth, keep you under their thumb, and maintain an advantage of superiority over others. Individuals with false confidence are polarizing, defensive, and critical of people rather than the subject matter. They possess a high level of secrecy, purposefully withhold information, and do not like to answer questions. They also move in quickly and segregate their victims to avoid outside influences.

On the flip side, individuals with authentic confidence will be transparent with information and open to hearing other views to increase their knowledge base. Authentically confident people are not afraid to talk about their shortcomings — think Amy Schumer, Maya Angelou, Dr. Phil.

When you detect a toxic individual, you know what you are dealing with and can employ a strategy. These individuals can have a direct influence on your performance and your success, so don't give them that kind of power. Keep them at bay and deal with them effectively.

Key Points:

1. It is important to identify toxic individuals, so you can protect yourself from unnecessary complexity, conflict, and immense stress.

2. Individuals with false confidence are polarizing, defensive, and critical of people rather than the subject matter. There is a high level of secrecy with these individuals; they purposefully withhold information and don't like to answer questions.

3. These individuals move in quickly and segregate their victims to avoid outside influences. If possible, stay away from them.

4. Individuals with authentic confidence will be transparent with information and open to hearing other views to increase their knowledge base. Authentically confident people are not afraid to talk about their shortcomings.

5. Toxic individuals can have a direct influence on your performance and your success, so don't give them that kind of power. Keep them at bay and deal with them effectively.

Chapter 2
The Power of a Mantra — "Nope, Not This Time"

Tris Thorp, a lead master educator at the Chopra Center for Wellbeing, wrote in an article about mantras: "The word mantra can be broken down into two parts: 'man,' which means mind, and 'tra,' which means transport or vehicle. In other words, a mantra is an instrument of the mind — a powerful sound or vibration that you can use to enter a deep state of meditation.

"Like a seed, planted with the intention of blossoming into a beautiful perennial, a mantra can be thought of as a seed for energizing an intention. Much in the same way you plant a flower seed, you plant mantras in the fertile soil of practice. You nurture them and over time they bear the fruit of your intention." (From "What Is a Mantra?" www.chopra.com/articles/what-is-a-mantra.)

In 2006, six years after my experience at the investment bank in Greenwich, Connecticut, and prior to starting my own business in 2013, I worked from home for a startup company. Once the company became more established, the managing partners leased office space on the outskirts of downtown Houston and began getting their processes and procedures in place.

The office had beige walls and floor-to-ceiling windows that looked out onto a parking garage. The employees and the partners sat in an open floor plan around a large square desk. The atmosphere was tense; you were walking on eggshells the minute you set foot on the office floor. You could hear every whisper, sneeze, cough, conversation, or phone call regardless of where you sat. You were always under the watchful eye of the partners, and they did not hesitate to let you know when you said something they didn't agree with or when you talked too loudly.

The two partners had distinct personality types; both were intelligent and passionate about their business, but their personal dispositions were dramatically different. One of the partners was jovial, witty, personable, and great with employees, clients, and candidates; she had an instant likeable quality about her. The other partner was controlling, secretive, critical — a know-it-all who showed perpetual dissatisfaction with the employees' attitudes, attire, work performance, eating habits, desk organization, etc. She struggled at building relationships and instantly gave off a judgmental vibe that made people uneasy. I would often hear coworkers, friends, candidates, and clients say, "I don't think she likes me," or "Next time we meet, can you please not bring her along?" You had to work hard to engage her, and, once you did, she would bore you with her accomplishments and vast knowledge of the commodity industry… YAWN! It was fascinating that the partners worked together so well (or appeared to, at least), given their opposite dispositions. However, they had been friends for many years prior to going into business together. They must have brought qualities to the table that complemented each other somehow.

Having a female-owned business in the corporate America is uncommon on its own, but having an all-female staff is virtually unheard of. Every now and then, the partners would hire a man, but they never lasted. Perhaps the management style of chastising and belittling didn't work as well with men as it did with women. Way to go, guys!

My least favorite part of the job was having a performance review every three months. When you have a formal review that often, it does not help you to improve your performance — it simply serves to put you on edge and intimidate you into working harder. The partners used the metrics to let you know they were watching you closely and knew every move you made. How many marketing calls did you make? How many client visits did you have? How many accounts did you get this week? This information was all logged in the company database and could be cross-checked by the partners, but they preferred to go over it in a face-to-face meeting.

Don't get me wrong, metrics are important and can highlight when someone is not pulling their weight; however, it isn't necessary to have a review four times a year unless a salesperson isn't performing. Once a year would be more than enough. The partners used the review meetings to micromanage, demonstrate superiority, instill fear, and create insecurity. They were both masters of moving the goalpost and enjoyed changing the rules to suit their needs. None of this made sense to me, as the company was doing well financially, and the business was growing at a fast pace. They were nowhere near the edge of bankruptcy, and there was no reason for this level of scrutiny.

This is how the review meetings went: The two managing partners would solemnly walk into the conference room, sit at the head and corner seats of the table, and hand me a three- to five–page document. They would go over each line item in detail, dissecting my performance metrics. The process was grueling and always took me back to being called into the principal's office. My mouth would go instantly dry, my tongue felt like sandpaper, and my neck would break out in hives. There was always an element of surprise to these performance review meetings, and rarely were they positive. The partners liked to blindside you in some way and to put you on the defensive, making you feel you had dropped the ball. If I made ninety-five calls instead of one hundred, the partners would focus on that; if I met with ten possible leads instead of twelve, they would go into lecture mode, or they would use this time as a teaching moment. The partners had strict targets they required each salesperson to meet, and the focus was not on the quality of the metrics but on the quantity. Personally, I felt it was more productive to make ten quality calls than a hundred useless calls. Metrics are a helpful tool for salespeople who are inexperienced or not generating consistent revenue, so that they can see the activity level needed to meet revenue goals. However, for a senior salesperson who consistently generates revenue, it's the equivalent to going back to preschool; a more mature process is required for a salesperson at that level. Therefore, the quarterly reviews served only to remind us of the partners' superiority, and the meetings did more for the partners' egos than for the salesperson's performance.

The partners' approach felt like a constant kick in the proverbial nuts, but I knew they weren't going to change, so I had to come up with a way to calm my nerves and get my mind under control. I tried wearing a turtleneck to cover up the hives and bringing a cup of water to sip to manage the dry mouth, but neither of these tackled the real problem; I allowed the partners to rattle my thinking and to make me second-guess my own reality. Their management style would affect me psychologically and emotionally, until my brain buzzed like an agitated bee. That's what I needed to address.

One afternoon, before I went to my performance review, I took a deep breath and said a mantra to myself: "Nope, not this time." I'm not sure where I got the idea to use a mantra; it just somehow popped into my head. I said the phrase over and over again, trying to channel my inner strength and minimize my anxiety. I anticipated criticism and knew it was part of the process, but I kept repeating my mantra: "Nope, not this time." My goals were to remain calm, listen to their feedback, and respond in a respectful, intelligent manner; I would not get rattled, I would make no excuses, and I would not get defensive.

The partners sat across from a very different person that day, and it was a noticeable change. It was as if I had an invisible force field around me, but the partners could sense its presence, and they were confused.

As we went through my performance review, I was careful not to make any excuses. I acknowledged any concerns they brought up and I answered them factually. I took notes, nodded to show I was listening, and did not allow myself to insert meaningless chatter into the conversation. There were a few moments of uncomfortable silence, but I said nothing; we just stared at each other. Although the physiological symptoms of dry mouth and hives breaking out on my neck were still present, I was able to display a more confident and controlled state of mind, and the partners were noticeably caught off guard. Whatever they threw my way, I refused to react. The partners looked baffled and concerned; they even tried working a few different angles to get a better reaction — or any reaction — but I remained calm and in control. They began asking me questions such as "Do you understand what we mean?" or "How do you feel about examples a and b?" I could tell they were uneasy with my lack of reaction and my measured responses. Their faces screamed questions like "What the hell is going on here? What is she hiding?" I admit it was nice to see them being blindsided and nervous for a change. My mantra certainly helped me. Having that one simple phrase to focus on helped me remain clear-minded during the meeting, and it made me feel that it was within my power to resist.

After I'd been at the firm for seven years, the partners offered me a partnership, which surprised and thrilled me. I skipped through the parking lot on the way to my car, called my husband in excitement, and sang along with every song that came on the radio as I drove home. I was finally validated for my years of hard work and strong performance. But a couple of months went by and I was still waiting for the partners to draft the partnership contract. I found it odd and concerning; their delay made it clear the partnership was not as important to them as it was to me.

Was I being impatient? Had they forgotten? I wasn't sure why it was taking so long, but I tried to remain optimistic and to carry on as I had. However, the more time that dragged on, the more I became disillusioned with my value and my position in the firm. I began to feel like a doormat and was gradually overcome with embarrassment. Why had I stayed at this firm for so long? Why had I put up with the partners' mistreatment? Why did I keep believing they would change their poor management style and fully appreciate all my hard work?

Unfortunately, during a business trip with one of the partners (I'll let you guess which one), it became clear that my promotion to partner was not going to happen. After a long day of meeting with clients, we were exhausted and decided to meet in the hotel restaurant to grab a bite to eat. It was during this dinner that I realized the partners did not want to give up any equity in the company and that what they were really offering me was just a more impressive title and a convoluted contract that would legally prohibit me from working for any other similar company in the United States or Canada for two years, should I choose to leave the firm. None of this was explicitly said to me; however, when the partners spoke about the future of the company, she did not include me as a third partner earning equity in the company — she kept referring only to the two of them. It became obvious to me that the partners did not truly see me as one of them, and never had. I would always be one of their handmaidens. It was never going to be a true partnership. It was a joke. It was a tease. They basically offered me a make-believe title of "partner," which would mean I'd have bigger revenue targets to meet, which in turn would serve only to pad their bank accounts and add more pressure on me. How magnanimous of them! It felt as if I was about to be crowned prom queen — dressed in a beautiful gown, expecting to hear my name announced, ready to walk up to the stage through the cheering crowd — only to find out I'd been pranked, and that someone else was to be pronounced prom queen instead.

That was the last straw. I was done. By the time we got back from our trip, in August 2012, I had solidified my decision to leave and start my own company.

Launching my own company was something I'd been considering for years, even prior to the false partnership offer, but I didn't have the financial means, confidence, or courage to act on it. However, after that trip, it became glaringly obvious that I was not going to grow any further with this company, so I began thinking more and more about going solo. I even registered an LLC with the state of Texas, The Z Firm, but I didn't do anything with it. I'd tried to register several other names, but with no luck — it was challenging to find an entity name that wasn't already taken. The company name was important to me, and there was no guarantee I would be able to get the legal name I wanted unless I legally secured it. So that's what I did. For years, the managing partners had had me under their thumbs, and they knew it. They controlled their employees like puppets, through fear and psychological games, but gradually their grip on me had loosened. Mentally, I had grown. I was stronger and more confident. Once the fear of staying at the company became greater than the fear of leaving, I had my answer. After that, the decision to leave and start my own company was easy.

The day I left the firm, I sat down in a conference room with both partners and I said a new mantra in my head: "It's just time to go." I must have said it a dozen times before I calmly told them I was leaving. In retrospect, it was a conversation that should have taken place years earlier, but I was debilitated by fear and self-doubt. It had taken me years to realize there was nowhere for me to grow within the organization, and so my only option was to leave. I told the partners I wanted to start my own company, that I wanted to see my name on the door. They appeared shocked and mad, but I knew that deep down they understood — they just didn't want to show me that they knew I was doing the right thing. Again, my mantra was my reminder that I was following my truth. When my courage wavered, I repeated my mantra, and it restored my sense of purpose, so I could go through with what I knew I needed to do.

After I left the firm, I ended up in an unpleasant legal conflict over a non-compete agreement and thousands of dollars of unpaid commissions. The partners refused to pay the commissions I had earned during my employment with them; at the same time, they wanted me not to work in the sales field for six months. How was I to earn a living? Did they think they owned the entire sales world? How could I possibly afford not to work for six months while they weren't paying me either? Although non-compete agreements are not uncommon, my contract with the firm was outlandishly unfair, and not legally enforceable. It was simply another case of the partners trying to bully and intimidate me into submission, but I didn't give in. We ended up in mediation six weeks later.

The morning of mediation, I leaped out of bed and chanted a different mantra in my head: "Suck it." I repeated it over and over as if I was obsessed with the phrase. "Suck it, suck it, suck it." By that point I could admit to myself that I hated the partners and harbored deep resentment for the years of unnecessary stress they had subjected me to. And still, I was afraid of the outcome of the mediation. The mantra empowered me to detach from the fear and keep moving forward. If I handled myself with honesty, dignity, and integrity, I was granting myself permission to stand my ground.

The first fifteen minutes of the mediation were the most unpleasant. The partners, a mediator, and I sat at a conference table in a large room with each of our lawyers by our sides. It didn't take long for the partners to begin their manipulation tactics and throw out false accusations.

Every time I heard an untruth, I chanted the mantra in my head: "Suck it." It was difficult to listen to the partners villainize my actions and utter comments like "I'm disappointed in you," "You lied," and "You betrayed us" — none of which were true. In reality they had nothing of substance to point to; they were trying to make me feel guilty for leaving the firm. They were angry that their former money maker would no longer be lining their pockets anymore.

Several times I was on the verge of losing my cool and fighting back against their slander, but I refrained. I knew exactly what they were trying to do, and I wasn't going to let their vitriol get to me. Still I chanted in my head, "Suck it, suck it, suck it"; this was a game of intimidation, and I refused to play.

After about an hour of talking in circles, the mediator suggested that we go into separate rooms with our lawyers, so he could speak to each side separately. About an hour later, the mediator walked into my room and asked, at the partners' request, if I would be open to meeting with the partners without our lawyers present. I felt confident and wanted to show them I wasn't intimidated, so I agreed. In hindsight, I should not have allowed the partners that courtesy; they were visibly more uncomfortable negotiating in front of my lawyer (who was male), and by separating me from my legal counsel they thought they could weaken my resolve and negotiate a better deal for themselves. I can't blame them for trying. In fact, in the past, that strategy would have worked. But not anymore; I had drawn a line in the sand, and I had found the courage to stand my ground. The mediation lasted for six hours, and, when it was over, I walked out of the lawyer's office with a shortened non-compete agreement and a nice check.

This meant I would be able to start doing business under my company, The Z Firm. I was happy with the outcome. I had remained in control of my emotions, and I had not allowed the partners to intimidate me. At last I was free of their bullying!

On the day of the mediation, I was faced with an unfamiliar situation — I had to openly challenge the partners' authority. They did their best to question my integrity by claiming they had proof that I was stealing their clients and company data to start my own firm. They also lied about what made me want to leave the company. Instead they implied that I'd planned to betray them all along. The partners not only villainized me, they tried to make me feel as if I owed them some sort of blind allegiance for giving me the opportunity to work for their company in the first place. My secret weapons that day were my lack of reaction and my ability to psychologically block out and ignore their attempts at dominating and provoking me. The partners were counting on me to collapse emotionally, but I refused to give away my power. And, this time, I prevailed. I was in an important war of credibility with two shameless, arrogant, greedy bullies, and I was not going to lose — not this time. I had found my courage, and I had my mantra, and I did not give in. The situation was more hostile, so my mantra was more aggressive this time, and it worked.

Fear, stress, and uncertainty are emotional killers that can destroy your mind's power. However, they can be managed with a little bit of resolve, practice, and a few psychological tools. Training your mind to act with courage challenges your psyche to take a risk without knowing the outcome. Does this make you vulnerable?

You bet! However, the combination of vulnerability and courage loosens the psychological grip that fear has over the mind. When you act with courage, you are taking a huge step away from fear and a giant leap into empowerment. Analyze the problem, retrain yourself to act with courage, and use a positive mantra. You will impress yourself.

Sometimes I will hum a song to distract myself from a stressful situation or during a repetitive task like washing the dishes. The humming helps me focus and keeps my mind moving forward. One of my favorite songs to hum is "MMM MMM MMM MMM" by the Crash Test Dummies. It is a catchy, mellow tune that is easy to remember and has a calming nature. When you find yourself getting stressed, try to get centered instead. Using music as a distraction can help you get through tasks like washing your car, doing laundry, writing book reports, or mowing the lawn. You can also use it as an aid during meditation to induce a sense of calmness.

While music can help your mind quiet down and refocus, you can go a step further by repeating a mantra. Choose a unique mantra that empowers you and makes you feel confident. It can be a one-word mantra like "Believe," or it can be a short phrase, like "I'm comfortable in who I am" or "I've got this." You need to find what works best for you, and you may want to have several mantras for different occasions. For me, short and simple phrases work best. I like to pick something specific to the situation, which is what I did during my confrontations with the partners, but you might prefer a more general affirmation. Below are a few quotes from famous people that also work well as mantras.

1."The creator of the universe is lining up things in my favor." (Joel Osteen)

2."Action is the antidote to despair." (Joan Baez)

3."Ask for what you want and be prepared to get it." (Maya Angelou)

4."I exist as I am, that is enough." (Walt Whitman)

5."I choose to live, not just exist." (James Hetfield — Metallica)

6."Action conquers fear." (Peter Nivio Zarlenga)

Key Points:

1. Don't let your emotions work against you. Find a mantra that speaks to you and makes you feel strong.

2. Mantras can come from anywhere, including books, movies, music, or the internet. You can also make up your own.

3. Fear, stress, and uncertainty can be managed with courage, practice, and a few psychological tools. Acknowledge your fear and proceed with courage.

4. The combination of vulnerability and courage can loosen the psychological grip that fear has over the mind.

5. If you handle yourself with honesty, dignity, and integrity, then you grant yourself permission to stand your ground.

Chapter 3
Using Objects to Reduce Anxiety

Bernice, the former VP of Human Resources at my firm, has a daughter named Hailey, who is thirteen years old. Hailey is a beautiful, bright, well-mannered, respectful, and all-around great young lady. She's a good student, has a lot of friends, and enjoys volleyball. She likes to express herself through her clothes, music, and social activities with her friends. When she transitioned from fifth to sixth grade, there was a noticeable shift in her emotions, and Hailey became overwhelmed with anxiety. Although school was more challenging, and the sixth graders had an increased workload, there wasn't anything that explained the level of worry Hailey was experiencing. She would stay in her room for hours and not want to go outside or play with her friends.

Bernice had numerous conversations with Hailey to find out what was causing the anxiety. Hailey said she didn't feel as pretty as the other girls in school and was afraid she was going to fail her classes. She felt hopeless. There was no truth behind Hailey's worries — they were irrational fears about circumstances that were mostly out of her control and did not match the reality of the situation. This went on for months, until Bernice came up with an idea. She sat Hailey down in front of the computer and looked up the word "anxiety," so Hailey could see that it was a normal emotion to have. After giving Hailey a good understanding of what anxiety and worry are all about, Bernice pulled out a turquoise bracelet. She told Hailey that the Indians believe turquoise to have healing powers for stress and anxiety. From then on, Hailey wore the bracelet all the time. If she felt anxious, she would rub the bracelet, and her anxiety would subside. To this day, Hailey wears the bracelet, because it gives her peace and calm. The bracelet solved her problem right away.

My son Colten had a similar experience with anxiety and found comfort in wearing a cross necklace. When the cross necklace broke, he put the cross in his wallet and carried it with him always. Colten felt safe with the cross. It was especially important that he had it with him at football games, lacrosse games, during a test, or when he was sleeping by himself at night. When he was scared, he would hold the cross in his hands and say a prayer. The cross held deep spiritual meaning for Colten, and he felt protected as long as the cross was with him. Colten felt that God was on his side, and nothing bad would happen. The cross made him feel closer to God, as if God was personally leading him.

Although Colten had a Christian upbringing, I was unaware of how deep his spiritual beliefs ran and did not realize that the cross helped relieve his anxiety spells. When he is feeling stress, Colten grasps the cross in his hand and squeezes it, because it makes him feel protected. Often, Colten will hold the cross and ask questions about what he could have done better during a game. In a lacrosse game, for example, Colten will ask himself about defense techniques and tell himself how to play better. If he has the cross with him, he feels he can be a better player. Sometimes he would ask for help with a difficult test. If he gets mad, he will squeeze the cross really hard and ask questions, or even vent. It makes him feel connected to a higher power.

As a child, I used to drag around a blanket that had a silky border sewed around it. I would carry the blanket with me everywhere while I sucked my thumb, and I would rub the silky edges of the blanket between my fingers. At night, I was unable to sleep unless I had my blanket. I called the blanket my "that" because my mother would always tell me to get "that," which I thought was the name of the blanket. My "that" soothed me when I was upset, tired, bored, or uneasy. I had my ritual — the combination of sucking my thumb and rubbing the blanket. I had to do both together. I couldn't just suck my thumb or just hold the blanket — they went together like cookies and milk. Eventually my "that" got retired, and my mom rightfully threw it away. It didn't take long for me to find a pillow that had a soft edge that I liked to rub, and I continued to suck my thumb while doing it. Of course, the thumb sucking was the ultimate soothing habit and took the longest to break. My dad even tried to put an awful, sour liquid on my thumb, so it would taste bad and I wouldn't want to suck it, but it didn't work. I simply endured the bad taste and voraciously sucked my thumb until I had completely sucked off every trace of the liquid. It's hard to let go of an action or an object that makes you feel better!

There are many objects that are believed to have calming effects. Turquoise, prayer beads, crystals, stress balls, anxiety bracelets, elastic wristbands, crosses, blankets. Consider the list below as a starting point and decide what item or material is best for you. It can be a random object like a Kokopelli statue, a Mickey Mouse watch, a material with a silky feel, a piece of jewelry made from a particular stone or crystal, or any other physical object that holds meaning and helps to soothe you.

Turquoise

Turquoise is a stone sacred among many cultures. It is believed to have healing powers, to grant wisdom, protection, and the psychological power of self-realization, and also to bestow many other blessings onto those who wear it. The color of turquoise represents many positive things, including peace, tranquility, patience, and luck. Turquoise is believed to have a positive energy associated with life and earth.

Prayer Beads

Prayer beads are used in various cultures for religious and meditation purposes. By holding the prayer beads, you count how many times you recite a mantra, say a prayer, or breathe while meditating. Buddhist prayer beads and mantras are often used together to keep track of the number of times the mantra is recited. Prayer beads are used worldwide and come in many different forms. For example, I used rosary beads in Catholic school to help me focus and to feel safe in times of stress. By using the rosary, I kept track of how many Hail Marys I recited, and the repetitive action calmed my mind.

Crystals

Crystals are another stone believed to reduce anxiety and stress and to open the soul to inner peace. Spiritual individuals use crystals as a form of therapy to bring about healing and wellness. Crystals, in conjunction with a mantra, are believed to calm the mind and body and to induce a state of inner peace.

Chinese Stress Balls

Chinese stress balls are believed to connect the heart and the fingertips by stimulating pressure points and thus affecting the central nervous system. The mere activity of circling the stress balls around your palm reduces or even removes stress, anxiety, and worry, and it increases brain functioning. Some stress balls are made of a foam material that can strengthen the hand muscles and alleviate arthritis.

Rubber Band Bracelet
Anxiety bracelets or rubber band bracelets can also be used in conjunction with mantras. If you put a rubber band around your wrist and snap it when you feel fear or anxiety, the small sting helps to focus your mind on what is actually happening and not on what your brain fears will happen. You can repeat the snapping over and over to remember something important, to reduce fear, and to snap yourself back into reality.

Anxiety Bracelets
Anxiety bracelets, like a Lokai, are beaded bracelets infused with elements from the highest and lowest points of the earth. The black bead on one end holds mud from the Dead Sea to represent your lowest moment, and the white bead on the other end holds water from Mount Everest, which represents your highest moment. By having the highest point and the lowest point on the bracelet, a sense of balance is created, which keeps your emotions grounded.

Fabric
Fabrics can have a soothing effect when rubbed between the fingers. Whether it's a soft silky fabric, a rough texture like the seam on a pair of jeans, or a crisp edge on the hem

of your shorts, fabric is a tangible object you can carry on your body at all times. When you start to feel overwhelmed, just touch the fabric.

Fertility God Kokopelli

The fertility god Kokopelli is a deity that looks like a humpbacked flute player. He's believed to control fertility by magically bringing out the spirits with music. The legend has it that Kokopelli carries unborn babies on his back and distributes them to women, making them pregnant. Who knows if this legend is true or not? All I can say is that when I was trying to get pregnant, I had a Kokopelli statue on a shelf in my living room that I would touch when I passed by. But after two kids in two years, I didn't even want to look at the statue. I handed the statue to my sister and asked her to please take Kokopelli away. Shortly after, I became pregnant with baby number three. Kokopelli doesn't mess around! Perhaps I should've asked my then-husband to take away the hot tub and the wine cellar as well.

Not all objects need to have a religious or spiritual meaning. You can use any object for any reason. George, founder of a successful hedge fund in Houston, shared a story with me that is an excellent example of keeping things in perspective through using an object.

George is a highly accomplished business leader and keynote speaker on strategic effectiveness, value creation, industry trends, performance improvement, and customer satisfaction. He has advised the U.S. Senate on the economic stimulus legislation and on many issues affecting small businesses. He became one of my most influential mentors and friends.

While looking for office space to start my recruiting firm, I stumbled upon a small office building in the perfect area of town for my clientele, the Galleria. I immediately contacted the lease management office and set up a time to look at available office space. There was one particular space for lease that had a tenant who was planning to move out. I walked in to see a fully furnished 1,200-square-foot space, with three offices, a conference room, and a kitchen. It had a simple but classy setup and was one of the nicer spaces I had looked at in my price range. The walls were painted a two-tone beige, with molding across the middle, and there was a TV mounted on the wall by the reception desk. The conference room had a long mahogany table with six tall leather chairs, and there were whiteboards mounted on the walls. I fell in love immediately. It was the perfect size, setup, and price for my startup company.

After I signed the lease, I kept going back to the office space to measure for furniture and try to imagine what was to be The Z Firm: Energy Recruiting and Outsourcing. I was so excited, I couldn't wait to move in.

One day, while dropping off paperwork to the leasing office, I stopped by the soon-to-be home of The Z Firm. At the time, the space was still occupied by a wealthy entrepreneur named George. I wanted to introduce myself and see if George would consider selling me some of his office furniture before he vacated the premises. I was not familiar with the hedge fund and had no idea who George was. All I knew about him came from the leasing agent, who said George was a wealthy hedge fund manager with a private plane and frequently traveled to Colombia, where he owned property.

I wasn't sure which office was George's, so I peeked into the office at the end of the short hallway. I'd guessed right. George stood up and greeted me with a courteous hello and a look of mild caution. He was not expecting me, so I quickly introduced myself as I moved toward him to shake his hand. I was nervous, because not only was I stopping by unannounced, I was about to ask him to sell me something. It's possible I was also a tiny bit intimidated. Everything about George was impressive. I couldn't help but notice how impeccably dressed he was — his clothes looked custom-made and his shoes were freshly polished. His various academic degrees decorated the walls, and on his desk was a framed photograph of George with his arms around a woman who looked like a Colombian supermodel.

After I'd muddled through my introductions, I tried to make some small talk to establish a rapport before asking George if he would sell me his furniture. He was nice enough to chat with me and even asked me a few questions about my business. It turned out that he had quite a bit of experience with small businesses, and even during our brief chat he gave me some useful information about revenue targets and productivity goals. I was thrilled to have a businessman of George's caliber ask me questions about my startup.

After about fifteen minutes, I felt I had taken enough of his time and decided to get to the point. I asked him if he would consider selling me his furniture. I stared at him nervously, hoping he would not say no. George chuckled slightly and said he would take an inventory of the items he was willing to sell and let me know in the next few days. I was thrilled. I thanked him profusely and mentioned one more time that I was a startup small business owner and every penny counted. Again, George smiled, then he politely walked me to the door. The conversation had gone better than I expected, and, more importantly, I had made a new professional acquaintance.

George sent me an email a few days later with an inventory of the furniture he was willing to sell, with a price tag of only $5,000. I couldn't believe it. Except for the furniture in his office and a few other decorative items, he sold me everything for only $5,000. It was the deal of a lifetime, and it took me all of three seconds to type "YES YES YES, you have a deal!" I was beyond thrilled. My new office, which I couldn't wait to move into, was now going to be furnished. Home run for me.

George and I kept in touch over the next several months, even after I'd moved into my new office space. He traveled frequently, so when he was in Houston for business, he was gracious enough to meet me at The Capital Grille restaurant and catch up. His vast knowledge and experience with small businesses is second to none, so I used my time wisely to go over my questions and business scenarios and to listen to his advice. Nothing I asked seemed to surprise George. He always answered my questions truthfully and illustrated his points with interesting stories. Over the next couple of years, he would become a friend and business mentor to me.

One afternoon, at one of our meetups, George was telling a story about keeping things in perspective. He is a pretty laid-back individual, and he told me his way to lighten high-stress situations is by wearing a Mickey Mouse watch. In business meetings, when people are being "outlandish or preposterous" in front of him, he simply looks down at his wrist and points to the watch. As George put it, "Usually the smarter culprits get the point!" He is now the owner of five Mickey Mouse watches, thanks to his grandchildren, nieces, and nephews, who keep giving them to him as gifts. Who knew Mickey could have that effect? But it doesn't matter what the object is. The point of George's story was that in a tense situation it helps to have something physical to keep you grounded, and it helps to hold onto your sense of humor. If you can do both with one object, so much the better!

Find an object that has meaning to you or helps you keep situations in perspective. It can be anything — from prayer beads and crystals to Chinese stress balls or a Mickey Mouse watch. I also know people who use symbolic reminders, like a tattoo of a loved one who has passed away or a Bible verse that has special meaning to them. Once I met someone who had a tattoo on the side of their torso of an island where a friend had died in a diving accident. Other people carry in their wallet a picture of or a handwritten note from someone who is important to them — something they can look at or read in times of stress. Sometimes it's those little reminders that help keep situations in perspective and lighten the tone.

Key Points:

1. Tactile stimulation can calm the nerves and help you maintain focus.

2. Find an object that works for you — a coin, prayer beads, an anxiety bracelet, rubber bands, Chinese stress balls, a watch, etc.

3. Symbols like a tattoo of a loved one or a special phrase written on a piece of paper can also give you strength in times of need.

4. Use an object and a mantra together to instill a sense of calm and reduce anxiety.

5. Objects can hold any meaning you assign to them, including personal, religious, or spiritual; they can also serve as a reminder to keep a situation in perspective.

Chapter 4
Facing a Situation with Complete Calm

I'm sure you've seen the T-shirts and posters with the quote "Keep Calm and Carry On," and variations on it: "Keep Calm and Stay Strong," "Keep Calm and Dream On." There is a reason these simple slogans have persisted.

One morning, I woke up and started my normal routine of getting dressed for work. It was one of those typical mornings when I rolled out of bed fifteen minutes later than I should have, so I was in a rush from the minute my feet hit the floor. I threw on a bathrobe, dashed to the kitchen for a double shot of massively strong Nespresso, and grabbed a handful of sugar cookies to go with it. I sat down at my computer and began answering emails. Doug, our bulldog, was sleeping at my feet, and the kids were running around like fire ants getting ready for school. In between emails I shouted out commands like a drill instructor, so they wouldn't miss the bus. Getting the kids on the bus is the single most important task of the morning, so that I can have some quiet time to get my workday started. Immediately after they departed for school, I rushed back to my computer to send an urgent email to one of my clients, letting them know my candidate was stuck in traffic and would be fifteen minutes late for the interview. After that I was just about to get into the shower when I realized that I hadn't sent my husband the usual good-morning text. My husband leaves for work an hour before anyone in the house is up, so I like to send him a text message once the kids are out the door and I am up and running. I quickly sent a message that read "Good Morning!" And I included a risqué picture of my breasts. It was not the most flattering picture — the angle made my breasts look like giant honey hams — but I knew he would love it. WHAT HUSBAND WOULDN'T?!

As soon as I hit the send button, I realized I'd accidently sent the message to Facebook. At that very moment, my daughter walked back into the house. "Mom, I forgot my violin and I'm about to miss the bus," she said. "Hurry, Mom, where is it? MOM! Come on! The bus is coming!" I panicked. I grabbed her violin from behind the dog gate on the stairs and threw it to her. She ran back out. I slammed the door after her and immediately grabbed my computer to go on Facebook and try to delete the post. My head was spinning, and my breaths were quick and short. I kept saying, "Oh my God, oh my God, oh my God." I couldn't remember my password, which is saved on my phone, and where I usually check my Facebook anyway. My computer battery was about to die, and my hands were shaking as I grabbed my phone to call my husband. I frantically explained what had happened. He calmly said, "Okay, I'm on Facebook right now. What do you think your password is?" I was screaming, "I don't know! I don't know! Oh my God, oh my God, I can't remember!"

I stayed on the phone with John for what seemed like an eternity while he remained calm and continued to try multiple variations of my most common passwords. Nothing seemed to rattle him, even though I was yelling at him over and over to please hurry. Panic and desperation were in full effect. John continued to calmly talk to me until at last he was able to figure out my password and delete the post. But even though the post had been deleted, it had still gone out, so I wasn't sure how many people saw it before John took it down. It was mortifying to think about.

My cellphone rang a few minutes later; it was my friend Robin calling to tell me a picture of my breasts had just showed up on her Facebook feed. I immediately told her I'd made a huge mistake and I was trying to figure out how to get the picture off the Facebook feed. Robin suggested telling everyone I got hacked. Seconds later, I received an email from my dad with the Facebook picture I had posted and the question, "What is this all about?" Although my face was not in the picture, people could recognize me from my neck and clavicles.

That morning, when I finally walked into the office, my face was white as a ghost, and I didn't want to talk to anyone. I quietly slipped into my office, sat down in front of my computer, and thought about the number of family members, friends, customers, and coworkers who had probably seen the post. One of my recruiters walked into my office to say hi, and she stared at me with worry and asked, "Are you sick?" Yes, I was sick; I was sick to my stomach that I still had to explain the post to my dad.

Remaining calm in this very upsetting situation was the difference between making the problem worse and dealing with the problem. John remained calm, which is characteristic of him; he was unfazed under pressure, while I panicked and couldn't focus. The situation would have been much worse had John not picked up the phone that day, or had he not been able to figure out what my password was. I would have just bumbled around in a panic, helpless to do anything productive. The post would have stayed on the news feed and spread to a much larger audience. Since my mishap, I have removed the function from my phone to text pictures to Facebook, and I find that I am trigger-shy in sending risqué pictures. Lesson learned.

The ability to stay calm during a crisis is a positive characteristic possessed by successful individuals and leaders across the universe. Doctors, athletes, actors, performers, politicians, negotiators, business owners, teachers, lawyers, and many others practice this technique. They prepare and sharpen their skills of tranquility under pressure, so they can be effective and deliver results in their roles. People who maintain their composure in difficult circumstances gain the respect of their peers and are admired for their presence of mind. You too can make a conscious effort to practice this technique and adjust your behavior under pressure, so that you can approach situations logically and not emotionally.

Key Points:

1. Practice composure, so that in extreme situations you are able to see beyond the chaos and find a solution.

2. Concentrate on steady breathing and practice using a mantra — for example, "It's going to be okay." The repetition will help calm your thoughts.

3. The ability to stay calm during a crisis is a positive characteristic possessed by successful individuals across the universe.

4. Tranquility under pressure will gain you respect, and you will get positive results.

5. Make a conscious effort to practice composure and to adjust your behavior under pressure, so you can approach situations logically and not emotionally.

Chapter 5
"I Don't Care"

One evening, after a long day at work, my husband, John, and I met for a cocktail to decompress and talk about the day's events. We sipped on champagne and nibbled on some finger foods. I began telling John a story about one of my friends, and how frustrated I was with the relationship. My friend and I were not getting along and were barely talking to each other. I couldn't understand how we could be at such odds when we saw each other only a couple of times a year. We used to be very close, but at some point, our differences became way more pronounced than our similarities, and it seemed that we could no longer agree on anything. I went into detail about how difficult my last trip to see her had been and how I couldn't figure out how to make the relationship work. I turned to John and asked him what he thought I could do differently. He responded in a tired voice, "I don't care." I was slightly annoyed by his apathetic response to something I was struggling with, but I shrugged off his response and moved on to a different story.

I began talking about another friend of mine who was having dating issues and was disillusioned with men. Time and again she ended up in dead-end relationships with men who were emotionally unavailable, and she kept wasting her time trying to change them. John nodded along and appeared to be listening, but when I asked him what he thought about the situation, his response was the same: "I don't care." My frustration was beginning to build, so I decided to move on to a different topic, one that I knew would get his attention. I told John I was considering getting a breast reduction and wanted to know how he would feel if I went down one cup size. John quickly turned to me with an alarmed look and said, "Absolutely not." Although I know John is a breast man, I was thrown back by his hostile reaction, so I tried to explain my reasoning — I was having a difficult time finding clothes that fit me well. However, John wouldn't hear of it. With a twinge of irritation in his voice, he spoke at length about how much he liked my breasts, and how my breasts were perfect, and they did not need to be one inch, or one cup, or one millimeter smaller. He reminded me that he didn't often put his foot down, but he was going to do it this time. I chuckled and promised him he had nothing to worry about. I clearly hadn't realized how strongly he felt about the issue. I was becoming irritated with "I don't care", so I had to come up with something that I knew he cared about. I certainly got his attention.

I was pleased to finally get a response from John that was anything other than "I don't care." We then started talking about one of my coworker's sons, who is extremely bright and can write computer code to make Bill Gates jealous, but when it came to his grades, he was a C/D student. I pondered why it was that he had such incredible technical skills but didn't do very good in school. Coding is difficult and tedious, and you have to really apply yourself to excel at it. Why wasn't he applying himself in school? John responded in a calm tone: "I don't care."

Here we go again, I thought. Whenever I spoke about something that did not involve John, his reaction was the same detached "I don't care." After several such indifferent responses, I was rather irritated. I put my glass of champagne down and asked him why he kept saying "I don't care" to every one of my stories. I was trying to have a conversation, and he appeared to be listening, but when I asked him what he thought, he was profoundly uninterested and refused to engage. Although John can sometimes be a man of few words, this was an entirely new way for him to respond.

Thinking back to that night, I realize that John had the right attitude. If the situation discussed didn't involve him, he didn't care about it. He didn't get emotionally or mentally invested in any story that didn't directly concern something or someone close to him. Other people's problems were not going to rent a space in his head. John was using a strategy that kept him detached from other people's issues, as a way to protect himself from absorbing their problems. This doesn't mean he didn't listen to what I was saying or that he didn't like hearing these stories — he simply kept a certain distance. John had no intention of investing time thinking about the issues I have with my friend, or my girlfriend's dating drama, or my coworker's brilliant but lazy son. While he didn't mind hearing me talk about them, he was determined to stay removed. However, when I talked about my breasts, something he cares about, John came out of his shell to engage and express himself. It made total sense.

Herb Cohen, master negotiator and author of *Negotiate This!* offers a great explanation of why getting too involved and caring too much can be detrimental:

"You should care, really care... but not t-h-a-t much. When you care too much and are over-invested emotionally, there is an increased flow of adrenalin which causes you to become doped-up and dumbed-down. This results in loss of perspective, impaired judgment and a focus on failure.

"So always try to keep your composure and a detached view — distancing yourself from your natural impulses and emotions. This relaxed attitude (a balance between irrational exuberance and utter despair) can provide a bulwark against the onset of stress producing emotions (self-doubt, anxiety and hostility) — a psychological shield between the ego and the aggressiveness of others. In short, your mantra should be, I CARE — REALLY CARE, BUT NOT T-H-A-T MUCH." — Herb Cohen, *Negotiate This!*

John's "I don't care" attitude fits well with what Herb Cohen suggests — it's only John's delivery that needed a little work, so that he wouldn't come across as indifferent to the point of rudeness. I, on the other hand, needed to distance myself from other people's troubles. That's the important tool John reminded me of that night — learning to set emotional boundaries to protect yourself from absorbing others' worries and negative energy. Protect yourself from jumping to help solve someone else's mundane problems when you have your own to focus on. Save your energy for issues that truly matter to you.

Key Points:

1. Set emotional boundaries to protect yourself from absorbing others' worries and negative energy.

2. Keep a balance between caring about someone and allowing them to take up too much space in your thoughts and mind.

3. Don't be a dumping ground for other people's problems. If you agonize over someone else's worries and circumstances outside of your control, you internalize their anxiety, and the resulting negative thoughts can haunt you forever.

4. Release yourself from feeling responsible for other people's feelings. You are only responsible for your own.

5. Remember what Herb Cohen said in *Negotiate This!* — "you should care, really care, but not t-h-a-t much."

Chapter 6
Get Off the Crazy Train

I have a girlfriend named Harper. She is thirty-two and desperately wants to get married and have a baby. Harper is 5'2" with long blonde hair, a beautiful smile, and the figure of a sculpted fitness model. She is intelligent, has a lucrative career in commercial real estate, and she definitely turns heads when she walks down the street. However, when it comes to her taste in men, she does not choose wisely.

Harper has a track record of long-term relationships that scream dysfunction. She is on the crazy train. The men she dates give her the typical lines: "Yes, I want to get married someday, I'm just not ready right now"; "Sure, I want to have children someday, I'm just not ready yet"; "You are my best friend and I love you, I just need to figure out what I want"; "Let's take a break. I am not sleeping with anyone else, I just need some time to think."

Harper refuses to recognize the pattern and learn from her mistakes. She is willing to compromise on every level just to push the transaction through and meet her goal. Most recently, after she invested three years in a relationship, Harper was dumped by a guy who had told her all along that he wasn't ready to get married or have children. While her biological clock is ticking away, her desperation meter is kicking into overdrive.

In an effort to expand her options, Harper decided to try dating outside of Houston. She met a military special ops professional online. Special Ops is thirty-eight, lives on the West Coast, has never been married, and does not have children. He is dedicated to his job and his country. He is attractive, has an incredibly sculpted body, a great sense of humor, and lots of integrity — all the things women salivate for. By all counts, he is a catch. After two months of chatting with him online, Harper jumped in her car and drove twenty-two hours from Houston to California to meet Special Ops in person. They had a wonderful weekend getting to know each other, having sex, and becoming intimate. Special Ops told her about his commitment to his career and how it has hindered his ability to have stable relationships. Depending on his assignment, he might be gone for six months or more at a time, with little or no communication. He is unable to make any long-term plans, which makes dating — and, indeed, maintaining any kind of committed relationship that requires him to be present — next to impossible. He is 100 percent married to his job.

Shortly after Harper came back from her whirlwind weekend, she called me up and asked me to meet her for lunch. She insisted that I come alone, as she was in dire need of relationship advice. I showed up ready to listen and offer my honest opinion, as I had done any number of times in the past. I wanted the best for Harper, and I vowed to tell her what I truly thought.

As soon as Harper sat down across from me, she started telling me how wonderful Special Ops was and how the chemistry between them was out of this world. They shared the same values, their goals were the same, and apparently the sex was to die for. Harper drifted off occasionally and talked about his job and how unavailable he was, but she claimed she was okay with that. I started asking her questions about his job and about how she would deal with him being gone for six months, with very little contact and her not knowing where he was. She was adamant that it would not be an issue. I'm not sure if she was trying to convince me or herself. She claimed she could handle his erratic schedule, but then she would waver and say how frustrating it was that he didn't always text her back immediately and sometimes it could be two days before she would hear from him. Special Ops was not allowed to text or call when he was on a mission or in training. His job didn't allow for that kind of communication — when he was on the job, he virtually disappeared. Although he had a legitimate reason for not being able to respond, Harper felt like she was constantly on edge as she waited to hear from him. The uncertainty was intoxicating and frustrating to her at the same time.

Harper and I spoke for two hours about the different ways she could make the relationship work. She acknowledged that Special Ops' career and duty to his country came first, and everything else was somewhere down the line. But she was willing to make that sacrifice. She was ready to come second to his job, because she thought he was worth it. In fact, she was already thinking about breaking her lease and moving into his house in California. She said she had briefly mentioned her plans to Special Ops, but I wasn't entirely convinced she was as transparent with him as she thought she was, and she also didn't mention how he'd reacted to her suggestion. Harper couldn't stop talking about her future with Special Ops and was already planning her next trip to go see him. He was unable to come to Houston to see her because his schedule was too unpredictable. When she told me this, Harper sounded a little frustrated about being unable to lock down a date. It's hard to get excited about getting together with your long-distance crush when you have absolutely no idea when you might see him next. There wasn't even a small window of time he could commit to with any certainty. To be involved with Special Ops in any way meant that Harper had to fly by the seat of her pants all the time. He might be there, or he might not. That was the best answer he could give her.

As we discussed a series of scenarios for the future of the relationship, I found myself getting frustrated with Harper. She refused to listen to or acknowledge anything I said that did not fit the plans she was already making. She kept trying to make all the pieces fit the way she wanted them to, no matter how glaringly obvious it was that they didn't. I decided to try a different angle with Harper and asked her a series of questions: Would he be able to spend special occasions with you, like Christmas, Easter, New Year's Eve, or your birthday? Would he be there when your son or daughter is born? Would he be there to see your son's or daughter's first steps? Hear their first words? Go to their school plays? Did he even want kids? What if you have a death in the family — would he be there to emotionally support you or go to the funeral? What if you get sick — could you count on him being there to care for you? Harper responded to every question with an optimistic answer: "I can handle it"; "I've been on my own for years, I don't need anyone to take care of me"; "He won't be in the military forever, and in ten years he will retire with excellent benefits"; "I can keep myself busy, I'm self-sufficient."

Harper had an answer for every question. The truth is, she already had those answers before she'd even invited me to lunch. She had made up her mind, and nothing I could say could dissuade her from her chosen course.

I agreed with Harper that it was a plus that they had such great chemistry together; it was a necessary piece of the puzzle for any successful relationship. It was also a plus that Special Ops was a man with integrity who openly admitted that he struggled with relationships because he was not able to dedicate the time needed; he had made it clear that his job came first, and that was not going to change. It's a life choice he'd made a long time ago, and he was comfortable with that. And once again I asked Harper if she was prepared to be in a relationship with no communication or physical contact for months at a time. Was she ready to deal with the inability to make plans for a simple date night or a family function? Was she prepared to be, effectively, a single mom? Was she prepared to be with someone who was never home? I reminded Harper that it takes more than chemistry to make a relationship work. For most people it would be impossible to thrive in the kind of relationship she was describing. Most people need more from a partner in order to feel fulfilled. In the end, though it was not what she wanted to hear, I encouraged Harper to walk away from the relationship before she'd invested any more emotional capital; he was not emotionally or physically available, not long term. Of course, it would take her some time to get past these feelings, but it was better to do it now, before she'd invested even more of herself in the relationship, rather than three years down the line when she had a child as well.

The red flags were right in front of Harper's face, but she found a way to ignore every one of them. After talking in circles for two hours, I was exhausted. I concluded that Harper didn't really want to hear my honest advice — she wanted me to tell her only what she wanted to hear. At the end of the conversation, she took a deep breath and said, "So, I should go see him again this weekend, right?" I just dropped my head into my hands and slowly shook it in exasperation. She was a lost cause if I ever saw one.

Two months after Harper and I met to talk about Special Ops, she sent me a text message saying she was moving to California. She was so excited. She said she had family in California and had always wanted to live there, so the timing was perfect. I hadn't heard much from her since our lunch, so I asked if she was still seeing Special Ops. She said yes — they were still talking, and she was optimistic about where the relationship was headed. If nothing else, I was relieved to hear she wasn't moving in with him straight away. I hoped things would work out for them, but I remained very skeptical.

Harper sold everything to move to California, including her condo, some of her furniture, clothes, and shoes. She packed what remained of her possessions into a U-Haul and headed for a twenty-two-hour drive to California. Shortly after Harper got on the road, she sent me a text message. Special Ops had called to tell her he was being deployed and he couldn't tell her anything more than that. He couldn't tell her how long he would be deployed for, where he was going to be, or when he would be able to contact her next. Harper was devastated. She'd just left her entire life behind, and now, out of the blue, he was gone, and she didn't know when she was going to see him again. Although I wasn't surprised by this development, I refrained from saying anything that would depress her further. I remained interested and positive but detached at the same time (thanks, Herb Cohen!). I had decided I would not allow myself to repeat the same mistake with Harper and become absorbed in her problems if she was not prepared to change.

Harper made it to California and moved into a beautiful condo on Catalina Island, with a breathtaking view of the beach, where she surfs and windsurfs. I'm not sure at what point she finally accepted that things weren't going to work out with Special Ops, but right now Harper is single again and still looking for Mr. Right.

Although Harper had great intentions, she suffered from lack of self-awareness, and she continued to repeat the same mistakes. Over and over, she invested her time in men who were emotionally or physically unavailable. She fell in love with a fantasy, rushed into relationships, and robbed herself of the happiness she was so desperately seeking. She caused herself more pain by dating men who had openly communicated to her at the beginning of the relationship that they were not in the same place as she was and didn't want the same things. And still she persisted, holding on to her fantasy that these men would magically turn out to be who she wanted them to be, as opposed to who they really were. A slight change in Harper's behavior — heeding the red flags and having the courage to walk away from a relationship that did not give her everything she was looking for — would have opened for her the possibility of meeting the right person. Had she recognized how self-sabotaging her pattern of behavior was, she could have moved closer to her goal of marriage and children. Instead, Harper kept hanging on, ignoring what she didn't want to hear, and so she continued to run in place. She was her own worst enemy.

We can all learn from Harper's experience. Smarten up, protect yourself, and invest your time and feelings into people who align with your goals. Recognize red flags, listen to the advice of people who have your best interests at heart, and do not allow yourself to gloss over what you don't want to hear. If something doesn't fit right, have the strength to walk away. Being able to do that is a sign of personal growth. And lastly, remain level-headed and patient.

"Whatever's meant to happen, will happen; And everything that has happened, happened for a reason." — Margaret Skipper

Key Points:

1. Recognize your patterns of behavior and learn from your mistakes; don't repeat them and expect a different outcome.

2. Have the courage to walk away from a situation that is not a good fit, even though your feelings tell you differently.

3. Smarten up, protect yourself, and invest your time and feelings in people who align with your goals.

4. Recognize and acknowledge red flags — they are showing up for a reason.

5. Ask questions, listen to the answers, and don't gloss over what you don't want to hear.

Chapter 7
Frame of Mind

Have you ever been in an argument where you ended up fighting about something completely different than what you originally disagreed about? You start arguing over where to go for dinner and you end up fighting about your boyfriend's laziness. Sound familiar? Sometimes the original point of disagreement is just a symptom of a larger problem and it just serves as a trigger for the bigger conversation. But when manipulative people are cornered, they sometimes use this tactic of distraction to frustrate the other person and get them off track. By saying things that sting and throwing irrelevant information into the argument, such people drag you down a rabbit hole that is meant to deflect the original issue at hand.

My friend Paige has an ex-husband who she refers to as Hades, god of the underworld, he was a master at manipulation and distraction. After they divorced, Paige and Hades communicated mostly through email and text messages, but neither of them were very good at expressing themselves in a way that the other person could understand. Most of their arguments ended in character assassinations and verbal lashings.

Hades had an aptness for provoking people and being antagonistic. In particular, he had the ability to get Paige emotionally distraught and angry to the point where she would lose sight of the original issue. He would call Paige at the last minute and say he couldn't pick up the kids when she had an important business meeting, or he would send her a text message that the water was being cut off in her neighborhood when it was not. With him, the sky was always falling. It was constant and relentless sabotage, and Paige fell for it over and over again.

After five long years of fighting, Paige did not have the willingness to collaborate with Hades anymore. She was worn out. She wanted to move beyond the constant fights, but Hades had a deep-rooted need to argue. He liked playing devil's advocate just to make the conversations more irritating. Confrontation fueled him, but their arguments frequently escalated beyond a casual debate or friendly banter. They turned into verbal abuse.

Hades made an excellent living. He earned a large salary, big bonuses, stock options, and had a lifetime pension. And then there was the boat club, the multiple motorcycles, the sports cars, and the golf membership at an exclusive country club. After the divorce, he custom-built a 5,000-square-foot house with an outdoor oasis that included a $200,000 swimming pool and top-of-the line outdoor kitchen. Hades was living large and spending his money on anything his selfish soul craved. Planning for the future, their children, or any unforeseen crisis was about to become Paige's problem.

During the financial crisis, Hades lost his job of several years. He received a twelve-month severance package, including full insurance benefits. He took some time off, booked a $10,000 golf trip to Pebble Beach, hung out at local bars, and lived lavishly. After a few months he started to look for a new job but was finding it difficult. Hades was in his early fifties at that point and had burned bridges, both personal and professional. He had a reputation for being argumentative, dishonest, and manipulative. He was a high-conflict person who was not only difficult to work with, he was difficult to get rid of.

After being out of work for a year, Hades had run out of money and fallen behind on his child support payments. He refused financially contribute to any of their children's necessary expenses or extracurricular activities — he kept saying he couldn't afford it. He tried to gain sympathy from Paige by pleading poverty and talking about how difficult the job market was, and then he started throwing accusations at Paige, to throw her off. A few years earlier, his strategy may have worked, and she would have lost focus and gone on the defensive. But by now she had learned to recognize when he was trying to provoke her, and she refused to let him do that. Paige sent Hades an email about his late child support payments, and when he tried to draw her into another argument, she remained calm.

The email chain below is a bit lengthy, but stick with it, because it's educational. You will see how Hades tries to get Paige off track by bringing irrelevant information into the conversation. He also baits her to go line item by line item in defense of the untruths he has thrown at her. But Paige remained calm and didn't address the irrelevant information, she stuck to the topic at hand.

The names of their children have been changed to protect their privacy.

Hades,

The objective of child support is not to take your money, but to provide for your children. As it stands right now, you've really put me behind the eight ball in taking care of the kids. For the last several months, I have been covering the medical, dental, and orthodontic bills that you said you could not afford but would pay me back for in the future. It's becoming clear that you are not keeping up with your child support obligations now that they are not directly deposited. This money is used for the kids' lunch money, clothes, activities, etc. If we cannot come to a satisfactory conclusion, I will have to get the state to administer the child support payments so that they can be tracked better in case I need to seek legal recourse.

Paige

Thanks for the note, Paige.

I don't understand it though. To say that over the last several months you have paid medical, orthodontia, and dental bills is nothing shy of delusional. What did happen is you paid 1500 dollars for a down payment on Chris's braces, which I asked that we postpone, as it was not dire to have them on at this time. Further I asked that we get a second opinion. You refused both requests. Hence, you had the braces put on and paid the bill and told me I owed half. I am in fact paying half of the monthly installments as of the first date they were due. You had a school fee that was supposed to be paid in September that is still unpaid. That was 800 dollars and as a result Tyler couldn't go on his school trip. Keep in mind I paid 2500 dollars for Tyler's horn so he could participate in band at a proper level. I understand you don't have the same vested interest in his band activities.

To be clear I understand what child support is for. Please understand how frustrating it is for me to hear from other parents that our children are sharing other kids' lunches because our kids have no money in their accounts. Do you know how difficult it is to have a conversation with someone who is asking me about that?

While it is true my deductions have stopped and the timing of your payments have changed it does not mean I have stopped paying you. In fact, you have never been unpaid on child support.

The job market is extremely tough and I don't have near the income I did at the time of this divorce. I am remaining hopeful to procure a job as soon as possible; however, it may be that I will have to file for a change in what I pay in child support as I have no income.

Hades

Hades,

I'm not going to address each of your excuses on a point-by-point basis. You are not paying your child support on time. As of now, you have paid nothing this month. So, yes, I am unpaid on child support as of now.

I have no problem getting lawyers involved in this if necessary. Remember, even if you file to have a reduction, that is not a guarantee even if your current income is lower. It is also possible that it could be increased even if I am not asking for it, but rest assured I will ask for an increase based on past and potential income, if the court feels that you have been paying too little when your income was considerably higher. If you'll remember, I agreed to below-state-recommended child support levels for three kids.

Paige

Paige,

I am not sure you read my email in the context in which it was written. I did not provide you with any excuses, as you are not unpaid any child support. What I did do was address your claim that you have been paying medical, orthodontia, and dental bills for the last several months, which, as I noted, is ludicrous. I also addressed the fact that you have bills due for the children which remain unpaid, and that I am faced with questions from other parents inquiring why our kids have no money in their lunch accounts. This was in response to your definition of child support and what it is used for.

For the record let's be clear about this: The child support you get was determined by me. The cap was 2100 dollars per month for 3 children. I agreed to 2,700 dollars per month so you could afford to pay the mortgage and the utilities and not have to move to a townhouse as you had mentioned.

I am aware those caps have been changed since then. If your lawyer believes he can make an argument that I should be actually paying more for child support (without a job, and with income over the last 5 years which was not close to what I made when we divorced) based on past and potential income.

Hades

Hades,

I read it in the context it was written, but most of your context is meaningless. The heart of the matter is that you have not paid child support this month, and you have not paid your portion of the other bills for several months. Child support has not been paid this month. Ergo, I am unpaid for child support. I agreed that I would pay for the kid's dental, orthodontic, and medical bills, and you agreed to reimburse me. You are required to pay for half of these bills, and you have not reimbursed me. For the record, it is not a "claim," as you put it in Hades language, it is a fact in the real world. The reality is that you are not paying what you are supposed to pay. It's really simple to calculate this. Look at your bank account, check to see if there is a check or withdrawal for child support. If there is not, you did not pay. I'm pretty sure there is no check and/or withdrawal for the current month, and we are more than halfway through the month.

Paige

Paige,

Please provide bills I have not paid for several months.

Hades

Hades,

First bill due – child support $2,700.

Paige

Paige,

You're being silly. You said for several months I have not paid bills and you have. If it is only child support this month, then just say that. Do not exaggerate the issue. If not, then provide these other bills you have told me you have paid and I haven't for several months.

Hades

Hades,

I already sent you a copy of Chris's orthodontic bills that I paid months ago in February. Attached are the invoices for orthodontic bills, medical, school fee, child support, summer camps, and driver's education.

Paige

Paige,

Don't know about Chris's medical bill. Tyler's driver's education without my consent... Annie's camps... without my consent... fishing camps... without my consent. You owe Tyler's band on your own. I owe braces against my consent and child support.

Hades

Hades,

Chris got sick. He went to the doctor. I paid for it. Now you are aware of it.

Regarding the braces, when the children are in my care, I have "the duty to support the children, including providing the children with clothing, food, shelter, and medical and dental care not involving an invasive procedure." I'm pretty sure braces are not an invasive procedure. Now, it does say that there is the "right to confer with the other parent to the extent possible before making a decision concerning the health, education, and welfare of the children." It does not say that your consent is necessary for a non-invasive procedure.

You were also required to notify the Court and me, by certified mail, of any change or termination of employment. As of now, I don't believe that this has been done. Also, if you have an unpaid child support balance due not paid from employment withholding, you are supposed to pay through the Child Support Disbursement Unit. I'm not requiring you to do this yet, but I have no problem taking this step if necessary. That way it will be easier to track your unpaid support, and I will have better proof should we need to return to court.

Paige

Paige,

Chris's copay is 25 dollars. Why did you pay 100? So now you want me to look back at all the doctor's visits I have paid for and notify you of half the cost?

Notifying you that I am unemployed? Really? You know I am unemployed, you sent my résumé to a friend of yours for an open position.

You are hell bent on saying I don't pay child support. I have until May 31 to pay you and remain current.

Why are the kids constantly without money in their lunch accounts and why hasn't the school bill been paid?

It is my understanding that I can set up child support through a credit card. I am looking into this. This way you can track this very effectively.

Hades

Hades,

The $100 medical bill is in addition to the copay. It is an amount that the insurance company did not cover. You are welcome to take this up with the insurance company. In the meantime, your portion payable to me is still $50.

According to the divorce decree, child support is due on the first of each month. So yes, technically you are deficient. This was not a concern when it was a direct deposit from your employer in two separate payments each month on the 1st and the 15th. Now it is a concern. The first of the month came and went, no payment. The 15th of the month came and went, no payment. At this point, you have not said when you plan to pay. Until you pay, you are deficient.

Again, according to the divorce decree, you were required to notify the court and me of a change in your employment. Rest assured that I'm well aware that you are out of work. You have told me numerous times. That's not the part that is of concern. The reason you are supposed to notify the court is for situations like this, when you decide to stop paying child support and go on fishing trips.

Once you decide to resume child support payments, you are free to pay them any way that you feel necessary. If the situation can't be resolved successfully, we will have to engage the state disbursement unit. By resolved successfully, I mean several months of timely and regular payments.

Paige

Paige,

I told you I was waiting for a check to clear. You have never been paid on the first of the month. I don't understand the level of difficulty you are placing on this matter. I suspect you are irked because I went on a fishing trip which was non-refundable and you didn't get your biweekly check.

Obviously you have a copy of the divorce decree which you are quoting. I have asked you for a copy several times. Would it be possible for you to get me a copy of this decree as we used only your lawyer for this? It would be helpful, and I will adhere to it as I have up until this month.

Hades

Hades,
You can get a copy at the courthouse for 20 cents a page.
Paige

Hades paid his child support the next day. The lesson here is that temperament matters, and, if you can learn to control yours, it can be your true secret weapon during a disagreement. You can't change your personality, but you can change the way you respond in any given situation. Hades tried to drag Paige into a war of words by throwing out statements about the kids not having lunch money and eating off other kids' trays. The statement was meant to attack and deflect attention from the real issue of child support and to paint a picture of their children being neglected. He changed the subject because he had no good excuse for not paying his child support on time. But Paige recognized what he was doing and refused to be distracted. She remained on topic and did not acknowledge any statements that did not pertain to the issue of child support. Moreover, she consistently responded in a calm tone, limiting herself to the facts. By doing so, Paige foiled Hades at his attempt to have an argument and forced him to address the main topic of child support.

Key Points:

1. Control your temper, and it can be your true secret weapon during a disagreement.

2. Ignore the irrelevant information to avoid getting off subject.

3. Be cognizant that facts alone do not paint the full picture of the truth; manipulative people leave out certain details for a reason.

4. Deflection is an underhanded tactic used to distract you. Recognize when that's happening and resist it.

5. Learn to recognize trickery so you can avoid getting frustrated. Keep coming back to the facts, and your opponent will be forced to address the issue at hand.

Chapter 8
Finding Strength in Vulnerability

When I was twelve, my parents divorced, and my mom decided to move me and my three sisters from Houston to Panama City Beach, Florida. I was shell-shocked that my parents were divorcing, and I didn't like that my entire family would not live under the same roof anymore. We moved into a three-bedroom house in a gated community called Bay Point Yacht and Country Club. Within the grounds of Bay Point, you could see beautifully manicured lawns with luscious green trees, colorful landscaping, and gorgeous golf courses. It felt like we had entered into another world, a world of large houses, prosperous families, luxury watercraft, and club houses. My family lived in the very back of Bay Point, which is where the least expensive houses were. We had a small one-story house on a quiet street with the worst lawn in the entire neighborhood. There was an abandoned, seedy hot tub in the back that was filled with muddy water, leaves, bugs, broken pipes, and frogs. The house had been neglected for quite some time, which is probably how we were able to afford it.

My mom enrolled my sisters and me into a small private Catholic school called St. John's. The students were required to wear a uniform of navy blue pants or skirt and a white button-down collared shirt. The classrooms had roughly twelve to sixteen students per class, and they were arranged with rows of antique school desks, large chalkboards, and a Bible displayed in the middle of each room on an easel. The rooms smelled like old library books and were kept clean, organized and tidy. There was a convent across the street where the nuns lived, a monastery on the other side of the street where the priests lived, and a small church on the corner where the students would go to mass.

On my first day of school I sat next to a short, bossy Italian girl with long blonde hair. I will refer to her as Lacy and she had the mischievous look of a troublemaker. She seemed more mature than the other girls, and I had a distinct feeling she knew more about boys than the rest of us did, and she had probably even smoked a cigarette before.

Lacy and I became fast friends; we did everything together. We were polar opposite in almost every way, but somehow, we clicked. We went to the mall together, spoke on the phone for hours, had sleepovers every weekend, talked about boys, hung out at the beach, and occasionally skipped school. Lacy and I told each other everything, every last one of our secrets. We even wrote an imaginary story about our entire eighth-grade class, including ourselves, describing what each of us would be doing in ten years; we distributed a copy to each classmate as a keepsake. Lacy and I were in charge of writing the story, so of course we tapped into our imaginations and created the lives we wished we could have, full of glamor and grandeur. I was a high-end fashion designer in New York City, and Lacy was a top psychiatrist who also lived in New York City. For some reason, in our minds, New York City was the only place where successful smart people would choose to live.

It all started one afternoon when I was fourteen and Lacy was thirteen and we were having lunch at a Mexican restaurant across the street from the mall. We started talking about what we wanted to do in the future. Lacy, who was originally from Rhode Island, talked about this charming little place called Boston. Her mother had a big painting of Boston hanging on a wall in her room; it had colorful scenes of the city, with street signs connecting the neighborhoods, paved brick streets, tall buildings, charming cafés, lush trees, and beautiful bodies of water. Lacy liked to sneak into her mom's room to look at the painting. She would make sure her mom wasn't in, and then she would wave me in to point out the different neighborhoods, shopping districts, and cafés she liked. Lacy raved about how charming Boston was. I, on the other hand, had eyes only for New York City and its bright lights. In New York City, you can be anything you want — even at that young age I knew that. It's a fast-paced land of money, fashion, entertainment, and opportunities galore. In my mind, it was bigger and better, and I was drawn to it. There was something about the vibe of the city, the aggressive attitudes I'd heard about, the busy subways, and the hustle and bustle that was wildly attractive to me. I could see myself living in New York so vividly that my mind would become flooded with fantasies and dreams of greatness. Little did we know that the conversation we had that day at the Mexican restaurant would change our lives forever.

That day at lunch, Lacy and I concocted a plan to leave our small-town lives in Panama City, Florida, and head for the big city of New York. Although we went back and forth between Boston and New York, we ultimately settled on New York because we thought there would be more opportunity to make it big. We made a pact with each other and swore to God that neither one of us would back out for any reason. Loyalty was everything.

The plan was that I was going to take my mom's van one evening, drive over to Lacy's house, which was about forty-five minutes away, pick her up, and then we'd head to the airport to buy two tickets to New York City. For some reason the fact that I didn't know how to drive didn't faze me. I was just going to figure it out. We were going to fly to New York, get a cab to a hotel for the night, and the next day we would get jobs. We planned on staying in a hotel until we had enough money to get an apartment. Of course, paying for our excursion was going to be easy — Lacy's mom had a credit card. Bingo! No problem is too big for teenage logic.

The night we decided to leave, we kept calling each other to make sure neither of us would back out and to confirm that our plans were still on. While everyone else in the house was busy, I emptied my drawers and packed a suitcase full of clothes, shoes, makeup, and hair products. I even stole some of my older sister's clothes because they were more sophisticated than mine. If Lacy and I were going to get jobs, we would need professional clothes, and all I had were shorts and T-shirts. Lacy took all the cash in her mom's wallet, which was $250, and her MasterCard.

I waited until about midnight, when my mom, stepfather, and sisters were asleep, and I quietly opened my bedroom window, which faced the street, and dumped my suitcase out onto the front lawn. I then slowly walked through the kitchen, snuck into my mom's room, and quietly reached into her purse and grabbed her wallet and keys. My mother's wallet didn't have any cash, but I took the whole thing anyway, except her medical insurance cards — in case she had a heart attack and had to go to the hospital once she figured out that I was gone. So thoughtful of me!

I tiptoed back to my room, quietly shut the door, and slipped out the window. I left the window slightly open, just in case something went wrong, and I had to sneak back in. My heart was beating like it was going to come out of my chest, and my palms were sweating profusely. I loaded my suitcase in the van and sat in the driver's seat for what felt like an eternity but was probably about five minutes. I was trying to get the courage to start the van and back out of the driveway, but I had never driven a car before. I had no idea how to even turn the headlights on. Although I did not have a GPS, I knew how to get to Lacy's house from memory. I counted to three over and over because I kept getting to three and not starting the ignition. Finally, I clicked a few switches on the left side of the steering wheel to get the lights on. Then I said again, "One, two, three, go." This time I turned the key halfway, and the air came out of the vents and music began playing on the radio. I turned the key a bit harder to the right and the engine rolled over and the van started up like magic. Although I had seen my mother start the van many times, I had never started it myself. My breathing was excessive, and I expected my mother to run out of the front door at any minute, but she didn't. And just like that, I pulled out of the driveway in one swift motion. It was surprisingly easy. I drove down the road for about five minutes before a car came toward me and flicked their headlights at me. I panicked and pulled over onto a side street. I jumped out of the van, ran to the front to look at the headlights, and then back to the driver's seat to test the switches. I figured out I had the high beams on, and I managed to adjust them.

I drove down the narrow winding roads I had memorized from many trips back and forth to school and friends' houses until I reached the guard shack at the exit. The security guard stepped out, saw my gate pass hanging from the front mirror, and then he pushed a button to let the gate arm up. He then stepped back into the shack and sat down to watch his television show. The guard had obviously seen me before, but he didn't seem to recognize me that night. Or perhaps he wasn't even paying attention to who was behind the wheel — all he cared about was the gate pass hanging from the mirror and his TV show. I'm surprised he didn't stop me. Maybe I looked older than I was? My heart was beating like a drum as I looked forward and gave a casual wave back. I couldn't believe I had made it this far.

The night was quiet and there were hardly any cars on the road. I was scared to death of getting pulled over by a cop, so I watched my speed like a hawk while grasping the steering wheel with both of my sweaty hands, focused on staying between the lines. I was amazed at how comfortable I began to get even though I was driving for the first time ever. I managed to cross over the Hathaway Bridge and made it to Lacy's side of town. I slowly pulled up to the side of her house. I got out of the car and ran toward Lacy's bedroom window, which was on the second floor. She was looking out her window, waiting for me. She waved and started throwing her bags down. I grabbed them and put them in the van, and we quickly took off.

Once we made it out of the neighborhood and onto the highway, Lacy and I could barely contain ourselves. We turned up the radio as loud as we could and sang at the top of our lungs as we drove down the highway. Before heading to the airport, we made a detour to the beach to check out what was going on. We cruised up and down Miracle Strip for a couple of hours. It was a road that ran along the beach where all the nightclubs, restaurants, and entertainment venues were. Cars were cruising up and down the strip with music blaring and people hanging out of the windows. Groups of men and women walked along the sidewalks sipping on large colorful drinks, laughing and having fun. Although Lacy and I didn't get out of the van, we were enjoying the freedom like two wild and crazy teenagers, which clearly we were.

It was about two in the morning by the time we made it to the airport. I parked the van in a long-term parking lot and opened up my suitcase to change into a more sophisticated outfit. I put on a tight black skirt, a black blazer, and a pair of black high heels. I don't know if I actually looked like an adult, but I felt confident that I could pass for one. I slathered red lipstick across my lips and walked up to the ticket counter to buy two one-way tickets to New York City. The ticket agent asked me if I was coming back from spring break and I quickly said that yes, I was ready to go back home to New York. She did not ask for my ID, only for my credit card to pay for the tickets. Airport security was a lot more lax back then. As I watched the ticket agent run the credit card, sweat beads began to form across my forehead, and I could even feel the sweat starting to run down the sides of my face. She was going to know exactly what I was up to and our adventure would be brought to an end right here. The two tickets cost about twelve hundred dollars. I had no idea if the credit card would even work, but the it went through without a problem. Forty-five minutes later we were on the red-eye flight to New York City. Lacy and I were in complete amazement. Everything was falling into place so much better than we could have imagined.

The plane was filled with businessmen and women wearing black suits and ties, carrying briefcases and newspapers. Lacy and I found our way to our seats and quickly plopped down. Adrenaline was running through our veins; we could barely contain ourselves. We were on our way to New York City!

The plane ride seemed to go by quickly. We were too excited to sleep, and, before we knew it, the pilot came on the intercom and announced that we were beginning the descent into New York City. A huge smile rolled across our faces, and we clasped our hands and let out a high-pitched squeal. Looking out the window, we could see what resembled a mirage of the New York City skyline, with a colorful landscape and monumental buildings. A few moments later, the plane made a slight left turn and the captain came on the overhead speaker to announce that the Statue of Liberty was right outside our windows. My jaw dropped in amazement. I had never seen a statue that big. It was early in the morning by this time, and the sun was shining right on Lady Liberty's face. She was breathtaking. I felt so close to her, as if I could touch her torch. Every detail in her face, her crown, and even in her fingers was vibrantly visible. She was simply marvelous.

As the plane slowly taxied to the gate, Lacy and I quickly pulled out our makeup kits, brushed our hair, powdered our faces, and lathered on lip gloss. The pilot jockeyed for position at the gate, then I felt a big jolt, and Lacy and I both flew forward. Finally, the plane shut down and the doors opened; we had officially arrived in New York City.

Walking off the plane into LaGuardia Airport can only be described as a surreal experience. Cigarette smoke filled the air, along with the incredible and invigorating hustle and bustle of people walking with purpose and a mad sense of urgency. Nobody made eye contact, nobody smiled, nobody exchanged social graces; it was all business. My eyes scanned the terminal in amazement. Everywhere I looked, there was a level of sophistication that I found intoxicating and attractive. Lacy and I planned to pick up our bags, hop in a cab, and tell the cab driver to take us to a hotel — a nice one. We had two hundred and fifty dollars in cash!

We walked through the terminal without a fear in the world, only the feeling of excitement pulsing through our veins. We were on our way to baggage claim when a man screamed out, "Lacy!" Lacy turned around, and I quickly nudged her arm and told her not to look, as we didn't know anyone in New York. A feeling of paranoia overtook me, and I had no idea what was happening. Lacy quickly turned around, and we both started walking faster and faster. Within seconds, two men who were not in uniform but had badges caught up with us. They stood right in front of us and asked, in calm voices, if we were Lacy and Poppi. I quickly responded with a sarcastic smile, trying to hide my terror, and said, "Who wants to know?" One of the police officers looked me directly in the eyes, leaned in, and replied firmly, "Your mothers."

Lacy and I were not arrested, but instead we were escorted to the back of a police car. The police officers took us to a precinct in downtown New York, where they sat us down and began a long process of filling out paperwork and asking us questions. I was surprised at how nice the officers were being to us, given that we had just been picked up for being runaways. They spoke to us in a respectful manner, bought us hoagie sandwiches, and didn't seem to be surprised by anything we said. I didn't really feel disappointed that we hadn't succeeded with our plan — I was still in disbelief that we'd managed to get this far. I was starting to feel somewhat comfortable with our situation when one of the officers turned to us and said, "Which one of you would like to call your mom first?" Fear came over me. My heart started beating faster, and I felt a jolt of pain in the bottom of stomach. I hadn't thought about this moment; I was so wrapped up in the excitement that it didn't occur to me until now how serious the situation was. I had given zero thought to what I could possibly say to my mother when she found out what I'd done. That's how the teenage brain works.

My mother describes the morning she found out that I was missing in a way only another mother can relate to. Now that I'm a mother myself, I think about it and cringe. My mother came into my room and noticed that my drawers were open and empty and that there was a note in the middle of my bed. I don't remember exactly what the note said, but it was something to the effect of, "Don't worry about me and I love you." I can't imagine what was going through her mind. My note said that I loved her and my sisters very much and that I would be okay. I also apologized to my sister Heidi for taking her clothes. Now that I have kids myself, I shudder to think how I would react if one of my children left a note like that for me and ran off in the middle of the night.

My mother then began running around the house, checking the other rooms in a furious panic. My sisters had no idea what was going on. Everyone was trying to make sense of the situation, and they were completely stunned.

Where could I have gone? Why did I run away? My sister Heidi quickly realized that the van was not in the driveway and that Mom's wallet was missing.

Making the phone call to my mother was more difficult than I could have imagined. I was the first to make the call, probably because Lacy's mom was too mad to talk to her, after she knew Lacy was safe. Tears immediately streamed down my face when I heard my mother's voice on the line. I began uncontrollably sobbing and apologizing. I could hear the fear and gratitude in her voice as she asked me why I had run away and told me she loved me. I was unaware of the emotional crisis I had put her through until that very moment. Again, the teenage brain. Her voice resonated with me. She didn't sound angry, she sounded relieved and exhausted.

After several hours at the police station, the officers drove Lacy and me back to LaGuardia Airport, where they escorted us to a terminal to put us on a plane back to Panama City. As we were walking to the terminal, we passed by a gift shop. Lacy and I still had two hundred and fifty dollars in cash. We turned to the police officers and asked if we could get a souvenir before we got on the plane. They were nice enough to agree and let the both of us go into the gift shop. Lacy and I had a field day and spent every bit of cash we had on "I Love New York" hats, mugs, T-shirts, magnets, bags, and key chains.

Although my mother didn't sound angry when I called her from the New York City police department to tell her I was okay, once we were back in Florida and I saw her face, it told a whole different story; her fear had turned to anger. As I walked toward her, there were no smiles or tears on her face, only a sharp cold stare. I immediately tried to disarm my mother with some charm, but she wasn't amused.

Me: "Hi, Mom."

Mom: "Hi, Poppi."

Me: "I brought you a present. A T-shirt that says 'I Love New York' and a key chain with a picture of the Empire State Building, which is the tallest building in the world."

Mom: "It's not going to work, Poppi."

Me: "I know. I'm sorry."

After my New York fiasco, I spent all summer working as a hostess at Montego Bay, a seafood restaurant located by the beach. I gave every one of my paychecks to my mother to pay her back for my ridiculous adventure. Lacy and I were forbidden to see or talk to each other, which we abided by for the most part; we snuck in an occasional phone call when we could. We remained friends and occasionally saw each other but, with the things we had to do, it felt like trying to pass through Fort Knox.

That fall, Lacy and I were zoned into different high schools. I began high school at Bay High and I was miserable. I felt lost, doomed, and unworthy due to the pain I had caused my family. My grades were horrible, and I just couldn't see a light at the end of the tunnel. I needed a fresh start, a chance to wipe the slate clean and start over. My self-esteem was in the gutter, no one trusted me, and I felt like an awful human being. I asked my mom if I could go live with my dad in Houston, and after several conversations with my dad, they both agreed to it. My dad and stepmom drove eleven hours to Panama City Beach to pick up my belongings and drive me to my new home in Houston. I fretted the whole way, wondering if I'd made the right decision or not.

Before I moved to Houston, my dad drafted a four-page contract mapping out the rules of the house. I had to agree to the terms set forth in the contract and sign it — otherwise I would not be allowed to move into his house. I thought the rules were ridiculously strict for a fifteen-year-old to follow, and I had no doubt I would fail again. If a boy wanted to take me on a date, he had to come to the door and ring the doorbell; if he honked, I was not allowed to go on the date that night. Although I had not dated before, my dad was forward-thinking and put everything he could think of in the contract. I was not allowed to car-date until I was sixteen. I was to be home by 11:00 and not 11:01, or I would not be allowed to go out the following weekend. My grades were to be As and Bs only. I would get $50 for each A, $20 for each B, nothing for Cs, and I had to pay my dad $20 for Ds; for an F I had to pay him $50, and I would be grounded until the next grading period. Up to this point, my grades had been horrible, mainly Ds and Fs, so I was doubtful that I would be able to bring them up to As and Bs. There were many other terms in the contract, but these are the ones that stuck out to me the most. I'm not sure why exactly I wanted to go live with my dad, other than the fact that I needed a change of scenery. I had worked for my dad in the summers when I came to visit him in Houston. I earned money doing secretarial work for him, and I enjoyed the responsibility of having to work, the structured day-to-day schedule, and the freedom the money offered me.

Dad lived in the Galleria area in Houston, in a rented two-story condo with three bedrooms. It was an old condo that desperately needed to be updated, but it was clean and in a great location. The condo did not have many amenities, but it did have large bedrooms, air conditioning, decent closet space, and two covered parking spaces. The kitchen was the size of a cubicle, with beige linoleum floors, and in the corner stood a dark green refrigerator that looked like it had been there since the 1970s.

Living with Dad was very different from living with Mom, there were very few luxuries. Dad had lots of rules, accountability, and an ear for lies that was that was damn near flawless. When I came home at night, I was to go into his room to let him and my stepmom know I was home and to tell them about my night. This made it difficult to stand in front of them and lie if I had been smoking cigarettes, drinking, or lying about where I was that night.

Money was tight at my dad's house; every penny was accounted for and nothing went to waste. You ate every last chip, you ate the heels of the bread loaf, and you saved any leftover Diet Coke in a can for the next day; nothing was ever discarded.

My father was a landman in the oil and gas industry and was still trying to recover from the 1980s oil and gas crisis, which reduced demand for oil and increased production, causing a huge decline in the price of oil. The oil market plunged in the mid-eighties to less than half what it had been, and my father struggled to find work.

My father enrolled me in Robert E. Lee High School, which was the public school zoned to our zip code. Robert E. Lee was one of the worst inner-city schools in the Houston Independent School District. My dad didn't have the money to put me in a private school or to move, so Robert E. Lee was the only option. The demographics were multiethnic, with the majority of the student body being made up of Mexican and Central American immigrants and the children of immigrants; at one point there were over forty different dialects spoken throughout the school. Lee was one of the largest schools in the region and it was also one of Houston's most feared schools — it had the highest rate of juvenile crime in the state and the lowest rate of English fluency in Houston. It sure was very different from my small Catholic school in Florida, where I'd had nuns for teachers and only twelve classmates. Here I was in a class of thirty students who may or may not speak much English and had no coping skills. Although I was out of my element and knew it would take me a while to adjust, I still felt good about my decision to move and I did not have any desire to turn back. I was being offered a new start, and I was determined to make the best of it.

Lee was gang-ridden, with a student body that came from very rough home lives. Pregnant girls, fights in the hallways, and the police arresting students for drugs or weapons were all fairly common sights. One of my most vivid memories from when I first started at Lee was seeing a girl who was eight months pregnant get into a fight with another girl in the hallway between classes. All the other students went crazy and swarmed around the two fighting girls, cheering them on and yelling, "Fight! Fight! Fight!" One of the girls grabbed the other girl by the hair and threw her up against a locker. The other girl was kicking and screaming while her arms were flailing around like airplane propellers. Gobs of hair were coming out of their scalps, and both girls' faces were scratched and bleeding. It was quite a spectacle. It took three large police officers to break up the fight, and I never found out what happened to the girl who was pregnant. It was a savage fight, and both girls walked away injured.

After my first week of school, I came home and told my dad my teacher thought I should try out for the drill team. My self-esteem was not in line with what my teacher thought of me, so I scoffed at the idea and told my dad she didn't know what she was talking about. My dad encouraged me to try out too, but I still said no. I had no prior drill team or dance experience, and I was positive that I would not make the team. The fear of being rejected was so overwhelming that I didn't want to even try out. However, my dad told me it didn't matter whether I made the team or not, and then asked me a series of questions:

Dad: What will happen if you don't make the team?

Me: I will be embarrassed and feel stupid.

Dad: Okay, and then what?

Me: I will never want to try out for anything ever again.

Dad: Okay, so you never try out for anything again, then what?

Me: People will make fun of me.

Dad: Okay, then what?

Me: I will feel stupid.

Dad: Have you ever felt stupid before?

Me: Yes.

Dad: Did you get over it?

Me: Yes.

Dad: Do you think you will get over feeling stupid if you don't make the team?

Me: I guess, maybe eventually.

Dad: Would you regret not trying out for the team?

Me: Probably, but I wouldn't feel dumb in front of the whole school and people wouldn't make fun of me.

Dad: What if you make the team?

Me: I won't, they will never pick me.

Dad: What if they do?

Me: I would be happy and popular. Everybody would like me.

Dad: Are people not going to like you if you don't make it?

Me: Some people might still like me, but others might make fun of me.

The conversation went on and on until I became exhausted from talking in circles. However, I noticed that the feeling of fear was dissipating, and it was not nearly as overwhelming as before. By talking through the different scenarios, I had gained some perspective, and, as a result, I felt less anxiety about the possibility of trying out and not making the team. It didn't seem as if it was the end of the world anymore. It was a valuable lesson — sometimes we feel fear, but we are not sure what it is exactly that we are afraid of. However, if we examine the fear, we might realize that the outcome we fear is not so scary after all.

That night, I didn't have any problems falling asleep. I felt a sort of calm. I knew everything was going to be okay, whether I made the team or not.

The day of the tryouts, I was nervous, but I was as ready as I could be. The team captains picked groups of girls to come up to the front of the room and perform the dance mix we had been practicing. I sat back and watched every move of the girls who went before me and I critiqued their performances in my head. Finally, it was my turn. I ran to the front of the room and got in my position. My heart was beating so fast when the music started to play. But I let all my nervous energy go and danced as if there was no one else in the room. Time flew by, and before I knew it, the moment was over, and the next group of girls was up. I thought my performance was okay — I wasn't the best dancer, but I also wasn't the worst. The whole experience was not half as bad as I had made it out to be.

That day after tryouts, I met my dad at a coffee house called JoJo's. He was waiting for me in a booth when I walked in with a hop in my step. My dad asked me how the tryouts went, and before he could finish the sentence, I grinned ear to ear and told him I'd made the team. He smiled and told me he was proud of me. I was on top of the world. It was the first positive step I'd taken in a long time, and it felt so good. A feeling of optimism pulsed through my veins as I relished in my achievement. I now had a small measure of success under my belt.

Three weeks later I ran into my dad's condo waiving my report card in the air. I had made straight As, which, per the contract, meant he owed me $350. My dad's face was as white as a ghost as he nervously smiled and told me, "Good job." He was dead broke, but he paid me every single dollar. I bet my dad wished he could renegotiate that contract.

Bouncing back from a challenging situation is a tool to be nurtured. When life gets you down, that is precisely the time to dig deep within yourself and search for what it is that you want to change about your situation. Did you fail miserably at something? Are you afraid of failing before you have even tried? What exactly are you afraid of? What will happen if you fail? Are you ashamed of yourself? Ashamed of your behavior? Whatever the situation may be, you can find strength in your vulnerability. Walk yourself through a list of scenarios and ask, "Then what will happen?" See how you feel once you've drilled down to the core of the issue. The fear will begin to dissipate, and you will gain perspective.

Key Points:

1. Bouncing back from a challenging situation is a tool to be nurtured. When life gets you down, that is the time to dig deep within yourself and search for what it is that you want to change about your situation.

2. Remind yourself that not all scenarios will pan out as you think. Reshape your preconceptions by asking yourself, "Then what will happen?" You will gain perspective and the fear will dissipate.

3. You are smarter and stronger than you think. Harness your negative thoughts and don't allow yourself to self-sabotage.

4. Sometimes you have to find strength in your vulnerability and put yourself out there.

5. Never underestimate the power you have to create a greater chance of success.

Chapter 9
Jump

I came to get down
I came to get down
So get out your seats and jump around
Jump around
Jump around
Jump around
Jump up, jump up and get down
Jump
Jump
— from "Jump Around" by House of Pain

My first job in the energy industry was at a company that was a spinoff of a much larger American oil company. I was twenty-three at the time. An administrative recruiting agency contacted me about a position for a trade floor receptionist. I had no idea what a trade floor was, but I knew how to answer a phone, so I was eager to interview for the job. If I was hired, it would be my first real professional job in the energy world. When I arrived, I told the receptionist I was here to see Mr. Glover. She told me to have a seat, and that someone would be with me shortly. As I sat in the lobby, I looked around at the beautiful modern office décor, watched the people coming on and off the elevator, and listened to people's conversations as they walked by. Shortly after, I was greeted by Mr. Glover's personal assistant, Judy. She showed me the way to her office. Judy was about sixty years old and very well dressed — not a hair out of place. She was the utmost professional and conducted herself in a very formal manner. Judy sat me down and started going over the requirements and demands of the job. After about ten minutes, she took me to meet Mr. Glover, the VP of Trading. Mr. Glover was an attractive Jewish man in his early thirties — about 6'2", slightly balding, well dressed, with piercing blue eyes. He had an intimidating presence but a kind smile, so I instantly liked him. Mr. Glover showed me to a conference room, where he sat across from me, leaned back in his chair, crossed one leg over his knee, and said, "Tell me about yourself." Mr. Glover radiated confidence and maturity. He began asking me questions about my résumé and previous work history. I was so nervous, I could hear myself babbling and felt my sweaty hands flying all over the place as I spoke. Mr. Glover seemed slightly amused at my nervousness, but he didn't say much; he just let me go on about myself.

After a brief conversation, Mr. Glover put down my résumé and began telling me about some of the challenges with the position. He said the position had a high turnover rate and was known for being a revolving chair. He explained that the trade floor was an intimidating place where a lot of money could be made or lost in a matter of seconds. It was an intense place, and stress levels ran high; bad language was the norm, tasteless jokes were almost guaranteed, and you might even see a phone thrown across the room. Having a thick skin was a must. I told Mr. Glover I was absolutely ready for the challenge. He stared at me in silence for what seemed like an eternity and then asked, "So, why should I hire you?" Without thinking, I said the first thing that popped into my head, a line by Richard Carlson: "There are only two rules in life. Rule #1: don't sweat the small stuff. Rule #2: everything is small stuff." Mr. Glover leaned back in his chair with a slight sideways smile, clasped his hands behind his head, and told me, "Well, Poppi, those two rules just got you hired." I'm not sure why my response resonated with him, but it must have convinced him that I was the tenacious and resilient candidate he was looking for — someone who could roll with the punches and mesh with his team. I was so excited he had picked me! I couldn't believe my rubbish line actually worked. Now, I had to perform.

My job was to answer busy phones for a trade floor of roughly forty people who sat within an arm's length of each other. The floor was very busy and loud, with phone lines ringing off the wall and employees shouting across the room to one another. Judy walked me around the room, introduced me to a few people, and showed me where I would be sitting. I'd be sharing a desk with another receptionist and answering a phone system called a turret phone, which had more than fifty lines. The turret phone was a trading board with a customized keyboard system. It looked like a control panel in an airplane cockpit.

On my first day of work, as I was driving down the road, I became overwhelmed with anxiety. Part of me wanted to turn back around and go home. I was worried that I had oversold myself and was going to fail. I had no idea what I was doing or if I was going to be any good at it. Pat Benatar's "Love Is a Battlefield" was playing on the radio when I stopped at a red light right in front of the office building. I leaned forward and looked up to see three giant towers. They were truly enormous. I grabbed the steering wheel, turned up the radio, and began chanting a mantra: "I CAN DO THIS! I CAN DO THIS!" I kept chanting the mantra loader and faster. "I CAN DO THIS! I CAN DO

THIS! I CAN DO THIS!" until the light turned green. By the time I was in the elevator on my way up to the twenty-seventh floor, there was a noticeable shift in my energy. I had changed my state. The anxiety spurred by my self-doubt had turned to eagerness and self-confidence. I was ready to start my new job.

I was to be in my seat at 7:00 a.m. sharp, pass out the morning reports, and prepare for the New York Mercantile Exchange to open at 8:30 a.m. I was not allowed to leave my desk unless someone was available to cover the phone lines. There were only two other admins who knew how to work the complicated phone system, so I had to ask one of them to cover the phones if I needed to go to the bathroom or get a drink of water. It was imperative that I picked up every call. When the market opened, every line on the turret phone would light up green and red. I would answer each line, get the person's name and company, and scream it out across the trade floor, then push hold and answer the next one. The phone lines rang nonstop until the market closed at 1:30, and then the mad rush calmed down. The rest of the day seemed to fly by; I was kept busy learning the company's processes and procedures and organizing my desk. Before I knew it, the clock struck 5:00, and it was time to go home. I had survived my first day. The position turned out to be a great fit for me, and to this day it is still one of my favorite employers purely because the job forced me to step outside my comfort zone and work through my fear. As a result, I met new people, developed new relationships, learned new skills, and inadvertently began a career in the energy business that has served me well. That first day on the trade floor was the hardest, but there were many other days during my time there when I had to work through feeling stressed or inadequate or out of place. But

I had to go through all those feelings of anxiety and through all kinds of uncomfortable situations in order to grow personally and professionally.

Tony Robbins, a renowned motivational speaker, professional life coach, and best-selling author of several books, including *Unlimited Power* and *Awaken the Giant Within,* is well-known for his idea of the personal power move:

Did you know that 70% of the toxins inside of your body are removed through the lungs? Breath is an essential element to life, and yet today we're using less and less of our lung capacity. Think about it. When you're stressed is your breath deep or shallow? You'd be surprised how often we hold our breath! Breath is the key to physical and mental well-being, and if done properly, it can boost energy, relieve pain, and transform our lives. To maintain your body's optimal health, your cells must be oxygenated through proper breathing. Learn how to breathe properly by using this exercise. Take 10 'power breaths' three times a day in the following ratio. (Source:

www.tonyrobbins.com)

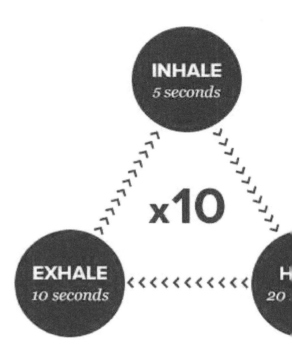

Action reduces anxiety. Whether it's by singing a song at the top of your lungs, jumping up and down, going for a run, pounding on your chest, or having a power-breathing routine, get the juices flowing, and anxiety becomes manageable. By doing something physical, you shift your energy, relieve anxiety, and allow reason and logic to prevail. Remember, personal and professional growth entail dealing with feelings of anxiety, so be prepared and establish a routine of anxiety-managing tools.

Key Points:

1. Action reduces anxiety. Chant a mantra at the top of your lungs, pound on your chest, or simply breathe deeply.

2. Remember what Tony Robbins said: "Breath is the key to physical and mental well-being, and if done properly, it can boost energy, relieve pain, and transform our lives." Learn how to breathe properly by using the exercise in this chapter.

3. Make Tony Robbins's Power Breath exercise part of your daily routine and take ten power breaths three times a day.

4. By doing something physical, you shift your energy, relieve anxiety, and allow reason and logic to prevail.

5. Remember, personal and professional growth entails dealing with feelings of anxiety, so be prepared and establish a routine of anxiety-managing tools.

Chapter 10
Kung Fu Baby

Kung fu, an ancient Chinese method of self-defense, involves striking blows at vulnerable areas of an attacker's body by using fluid movements of the hands and legs. The art of kung fu is much more than a self-defense technique. It takes years of training, discipline, fortitude, and patience to master the art. A fluid connection between mind, body, and soul must be present to create balance, depth, dimension, and understanding.

Rarely in my career have I had a client rescind an offer to a candidate with a signed offer letter in hand, but it does happen. It's a horrible situation for the candidate to go through, and it puts a blemish on my company's reputation as the recruiter. When situations like this arise, it's imperative to remain in control and follow protocol with integrity and compassion. You are delivering unpleasant news that will no doubt cause grief and frustration to everyone involved.

I received a call from Carol, a candidate I had previously worked with. She had landed a controller position at an exploration and production company, and she was in desperate need of three accountants who could start on short notice.

Carol was desperate. She was new to the company, and she had inherited a group of unqualified accountants. She needed to clean up the accounting group and do a complete reorganization. Her team had not been trained properly and lacked the skillset to perform the job functions effectively.

By the sound of it, they should have never been in these roles to begin with, but the company was trying to save costs by hiring less experienced people. The group was in disarray, and Carol was given complete authority to turn it into a lean mean producing machine. She had her work cut out for her.

I was confident I had enough competent accountants for the three positions Carol was looking to fill. I quickly gathered a handful of qualified candidates and submitted them to Carol for review. She immediately began interviewing them, and within a week she had a shortlist for the second round of interviews.

Carol was pleased with the selection of candidates and was feeling more confident by the day. She narrowed down the pool and made offers to three candidates. The first candidate received a counteroffer from another company for significantly more money, so he turned down Carol's offer. The second candidate accepted Carol's offer, but unfortunately did not pass the background check and was discovered to be lying about her degree. The third candidate accepted the offer. His credentials checked out, and he passed with flying colors the background check, credit check, drug test, and reference checks. Before long, he had an executed offer letter in hand, so he resigned from his current position.

Around this time, one of my employees, whom we will call Jordan, resigned from The Z Firm, stating that she wanted to spend time with her family over the summer and did not feel it would be appropriate to sit on the payroll. My business partner at the time, Brent Price, and I completely understood; we wished Jordan well, paid her the commissions she had earned, and had a going-away lunch with the team.

A couple of weeks after Jordan left the firm, some disturbing information surfaced that she had possibly stolen data from The Z Firm and started her own recruiting firm. I never suspected Jordan to have any intention of starting her own firm and was caught completely off guard. Jordan was a longtime friend, and Brent and I had trusted her with highly confidential information. She had access to all clients, contracts, and candidates' information. After investigating further, we discovered that Jordan had started a firm a year earlier, while she was still working for The Z Firm. Jordan was pushing deals through other recruiters but using our database and resources to do so, and we were paying her the entire time. Not only was she outright dishonest, she had stolen from us. Brent and I were flabbergasted and stunned. We were too trusting and had let our guard down. Now we were faced with launching a full investigation and possible legal action. Although Jordan's actions were no doubt sleazy, we had to prove they were also illegal. The situation continued to snowball from there.

Meanwhile, Carol still had two roles left to fill, so she continued to interview additional candidates. A week later she sent me an email telling me she had filled the other two accounting positions through another recruiter. Apparently, unbeknownst to Carol, Human Resources had recently started working with a new recruiting firm, and Carol hadn't realized that the résumés were not coming from my firm. I found that odd since everything sent over has The Z Firm logo prominently displayed. Turns out, the new recruiting firm that Human Resources was working with was Jordan's.

A few days later, I received an email from Carol stating she needed to delay my candidate's start date by two weeks due to an internal issue. The following week, Carol sent another email stating that she needed to rescind the offer due to an unforeseen legal issue with an employee. She was barely apologetic; she sounded rather matter-of-fact. I found it odd that Carol didn't pick up the phone and call me. Why would she email such sensitive, important information? It's not like she was rescheduling a lunch — she was changing the candidate's future. The situation was not good. I had gone from three placements to zero, and the way it had happened left a bad taste in my mouth. Carol asked me to relay the information to my candidate and wish him well in his future endeavors. Her message sounded cold and insensitive, which didn't sit well with me. Before I said anything to my candidate, I wanted to meet with Carol face to face; the situation was too important not to.

I requested an in-person meeting with Carol to get clarity as to why the offer had been rescinded. She was very accommodating and professional, and we scheduled a time to meet.

As I walked in the building, I quietly said a mantra: "Let's find the truth, let's make this right." I approached with an open attitude and a pleasant but professional demeanor.

When I arrived, Carol shook my hand and led me into a conference room, where the VP of Human Resources was sitting at the end of a long table. I shook her hand and took a seat across the table. We made some small talk. I thanked them for taking the time to meet with me and then I got down to business. I told Carol that although I didn't know her very well, in the short time I had worked with her she had presented herself as a woman of great integrity, and I was confident we could resolve the issue with the same level of integrity. I began asking questions. "This is an unusual situation for all of us. Will you please start from the beginning and tell me what exactly happened to make you rescind the offer?" Carol remained vague, if somewhat apologetic. She said her hands were tied and there was nothing she could do. As I continued to ask questions, I couldn't help noticing that Carol seemed nervous and couldn't really give a clear answer as to why this happened. She just said the same thing over and over: "I'm sorry, that's all I have." I felt unsatisfied, because she failed to give me any real explanation as to why she rescinded the offer. The VP of Human Resources was visibly uncomfortable and worried, but she barely spoke during the meeting.

The situation just didn't make sense to me, so I continued to press Carol, but I wasn't getting anywhere. I explained to Carol how unfortunate the situation was, not just for my firm but for the candidate. My candidate was in dire need of the job and had turned down another offer to take the job with Carol. He was the sole provider for his family and was having a difficult time with the downturn in the energy business. Carol sat with a stern face but seemed to have trouble maintaining eye contact. Needless to say, the meeting didn't last long. It didn't need to. It became clear to me that Jordan, my ex-employee, was behind the whole thing; she had intervened and sabotaged the offer to my candidate in an effort to slip her candidate in his place. Jordan was trying to make money by playing dirty. She must have downloaded my candidate database and stolen my clients' info while she was still working at The Z Firm, and she used that information to start her own firm. In the beginning Carol wouldn't have known that Jordan was no longer my employee, which is where the confusion came for her. Still, I was shocked and disappointed that Carol would stand for something like that, once she discovered what Jordan had done. After all, she was a high-level executive, playing with a dirty rotten scoundrel like Jordan.

That moment was very telling for me. Jordan clearly had no integrity, but more disappointing was that Carol displayed no integrity either. Why would a professional at her level act like that?

I speculated that Jordan had most likely badmouthed my candidates and then offered Carol an extremely discounted fee for using her as the recruiter on the roles. Was this business savvy? Perhaps. However, stabbing your coworkers in the back is not a way to get ahead and shows poor character. Yes, Jordan managed to get three placements in the short term, but it's not a way to build a long-term relationship. Clients don't like to do business with people they can't trust.

I left Carol's office disappointed but clear on where I stood. Although I gave the situation my best efforts, I could not change the outcome. It was not illegal for Carol to rescind the offer, but it was unprofessional and damaging to the candidate. I immediately called my candidate and delivered the bad news. He was understandably angry, but I could also hear the despair seeping through his voice; he didn't know how he was going to tell his wife. I expressed my sincere apologies and vowed to find him another position. My entire team would work on his behalf to place him at an organization with quality people and higher moral standards. Carol certainly showed her lack of character, and that was not going to change; it was better for my candidate to find this out now, rather than later down the road.

Although I didn't get the outcome I was hoping for, I got what I was looking for, which was peace of mind. I approached the situation with benevolence and gave Carol the opportunity to do the right thing. She did not handle herself with dignity and showed no inner strength throughout the process. Clearly, Carol had some work to do on developing her integrity.

Just like in kung fu, in order to improve and to grow, you must spend time developing your skills. It doesn't happen immediately — it's a process of trial and error that slowly moves you closer to inner strength. The kung fu philosophy teaches compassion, tolerance, strength, and character. In a demanding situation, it is these principles that will enable you to handle yourself with grace and create a positive outcome.

By approaching every person, group, or situation with benevolence, you change the tone of the interaction and remain in control of your emotions. Your goal is to face any situation with complete calm and use the techniques kung fu teaches to respond with kindness, integrity, compassion, modesty, and wisdom. It's the Yin and the Yang; soft and hard; good and bad; up and down — you get the idea. It's the balance. If you have achieved balance, then you have peace.

Integrity and standards are vital, both in personal and in professional relationships. Stand for what you believe in, demonstrate confidence, and approach with benevolence. Make benevolence a part of your core principles. Train your mind to respond with compassion. If you get angry, feel the anger, acknowledge what is making you mad, but don't act out of anger. This is the time to use a breathing exercise to help you calm down and regain control: Take a deep breath and then slowly let it out. Repeat. Say your mantra. Maintain your integrity.

Key Points:

1. Remember the teachings of kung fu and respond with benevolence. By approaching every person, group, or situation with benevolence, you change the tone of the interaction and remain in control of your emotions.

2. You might not always get the outcome you want, but you are more resilient than you think, and there will be other opportunities that will go your way.

3. Your goal is to face any situation with complete calm and to follow the principles of kung fu: respond with kindness, integrity, compassion, modesty, and wisdom.

4. Train your mind to respond with compassion, so you can maintain balance and peace of mind.

5. Know that there are dishonest people out there and sometimes you won't be able to avoid them. Do not let them derail you from your path. Apply your techniques and maintain your integrity.

Chapter 11
Anxiety Is the Devil in Disguise

Anxiety comes in many different forms and it can manifest in various ways. One type of anxiety I often see in my line of work is test anxiety. It's exactly what it sounds like — the fear that you're going to fail an important exam, which in turn prevents you from performing as well on the exam as you otherwise would have. It's ironic that the fear of failure makes you more likely to fail, but such is the nature of anxiety.

One of my clients, a large global bank, has an interview process that candidates loathe. Not only is the interview process grueling and long, but they also require candidates to take an assessment test. The first interview is a quick meet-and-greet with Human Resources or a hiring manager that lasts no longer than forty-five minutes. If that goes well, the next step is to schedule a date to take the test, which usually runs anywhere from two to four hours and must be taken alone in a conference room. Candidates are to dress comfortably and bring two forms of ID. The company requires every candidate to take this exam, regardless of their professional level.

Jack, a candidate I met when he was in his early thirties, was looking to progress his career by taking on a more challenging role with leadership responsibilities. He had ten years of experience working at an innovative private trading firm in Houston, a Bachelor of Business Administration degree in Finance from a Tier 1 school, a GPA of 3.7, and stellar references from his former colleagues, supervisors, and peers. Although he had been consistently promoted throughout his career, he felt he had reached a plateau at his current company and that there was no more room for growth.

The client was impressed with Jack's résumé and invited him to come in for an interview. He showed up for the first interview and it went swimmingly; both the client and the candidate had positive feedback. The client decided to schedule Jack for the assessment test and provided him with sample questions to review. Jack studied the sample questions and felt confident. The day before the test, Jack called me to say he was worried about it. He had heard from other people in the industry that the test was very difficult, known for having a high failure rate. I explained that it covered multiple areas, including cultural fit, personality, quantitative skills, and management abilities. The test was not something he could study for or take a crash course on; it was mostly designed to assess aptitude and personality — two things you can't really cram for. Although the company said it was not pass-or-fail assessment, it pretty much was. The company was looking for high-aptitude candidates with strong quantitative abilities who would fit in with the culture and become top performers in their roles. There are several other investment banks and trading companies that undergo a similar assessment process, but they usually assess high-level executives such as directors, managers, senior VPs, executive VPs, controllers, traders, etc. This firm gives the test to everyone, regardless of what position they are applying for.

The day of the exam, Jack showed up fifteen minutes early. The receptionist escorted him to a conference room. On the table was a bottle of water, a calculator, a pencil, and the test packet. The receptionist asked Jack to put his cellphone and keys in a basket, and then explained that once the test started, he was not allowed to leave the room for any reason until he was finished. Jack opened his packet, and about forty-five minutes into it, he walked out. Although I had spoken to Jack the day before, I had no idea how Jack was feeling that day. I told him to call me once he finished to let me know how the process had gone.

About ten minutes after Jack left the office, I received a call from the director of Human Resources. I could sense something wasn't right by the tone of her voice. She was very direct and said she was not allowed to discuss Jack's results, but they would not be moving forward with him as a potential candidate. Naturally, I pressed for more information, but she remained vague. I hung up and called Jack immediately. He answered in a low, irritated tone. I said I was surprised that he would be done so soon and asked him how it went. Jack got angry and said it was a ridiculous test, and that the job wasn't worth going through such a process. After several minutes, Jack calmed down and apologized. He said he felt nauseous before the test began and panicked when he came across questions he hadn't studied since collage.

Jack had answered the first five questions on the assessment test, and then he came across a series of questions on interest rates and exchange rates. He decided at that point that he was going to fail, so instead of continuing, he bubbled in the words F U C K – Y O U and walked out.

Jack let the stress take over his logic and temporarily erase his intelligence. He couldn't focus, and he feared the embarrassment of failing. What Jack forgot, even though I tried to tell him, was that the test measured multiple areas — it wasn't all interest rate questions. Even if he had gotten the entire section about interest rates wrong, he still could have done well overall and ended up with a positive outcome. Education and specific areas of expertise are not the key factors for success here. I have had PhDs who did not move forward to the next step after completing the test. It's not that Jack wasn't smart enough, it's that he made himself believe he wasn't going to do well, and he shut down. Even though Jack couldn't answer the questions about interest rates, he still could have passed. In hindsight, Jack admits he succumbed to the fear of failing, and his instinctive reaction was to flee. What he needed to do instead was clear his mind and realize that the best part about taking a test is that it gives you a chance to see your areas of weakness. Only then can you begin to improve.

Psychologist Carol Dweck, author of *Mindset: The New Psychology of Success,* researched and wrote about a theory of self-perception or "self-theory" that people hold. Believing that you are either intelligent or unintelligent is a simple example of a mindset. People may also have a mindset related to their personal or professional lives — "I'm a good teacher" or "I'm a bad parent," for example.

Dweck distinguishes between two mindsets, "fixed" and "growth." "In a fixed mindset," she writes, "people believe their basic qualities, like their intelligence or talent, are simply fixed traits. They spend their time documenting their intelligence or talent instead of developing them. They also believe that talent alone creates success — without effort."

On the other hand, Dweck says, "In a growth mindset, people believe that their most basic abilities can be developed through dedication and hard work — brains and talent are just the starting point. This view creates a love of learning and a resilience that is essential for great accomplishment."

Jack's mindset was fixed. He believed that he wasn't smart enough or qualified enough to pass the required test, so he didn't even try. His thought process was not set up for growth but for failure. Without a growth mindset, we are all just running in place. Don't be like Jack. Have the courage to take the test and deal with the results. You may fail on the first try, but there is always another time, another place, or another route to get where you want to be.

Some of the most prominent and respected politicians have failed the most important test in the legal world, the bar exam. However, they went on to have highly successful careers. Jerry Brown, former attorney general of California and currently the governor, failed the bar on the first try but he passed the second time. Hillary Clinton, presidential nominee in the 2016 election and former first lady, failed the D.C. bar on her first try, went for a second try, and passed the Arkansas bar exam. John F. Kennedy, Jr., son of President Kennedy, failed the bar exam twice before passing it on the third try. Emily Pataki, daughter of former New York governor Georg Pataki, failed the bar the first time and passed on the second try. Peter Wilson, former California governor, failed the bar exam three times before passing on his fourth try. Paulina Bandy of Orange County, California, failed the bar exam thirteen times before finally passing it on the fourteenth try. Had these individuals had a fixed mindset, they would have put in no effort to try over and over. It was the combination of talent plus effort that led all of them to pass the bar exam... eventually.

A heightened sense of anxiety only increases one's fear of failure. Use Dweck's idea of a growth mindset and apply the formula of talent plus effort to get the best outcome.

"Remember, even if at first you don't succeed, try, try, try again. Or, in Paulina Bandy's case, try, try, try, try, try, try, try, try, try, try, try, try, try, try again!" – *David Lat*

Key Points:

1. Remember Dweck's two mindsets, "fixed" and "growth." "In a fixed mindset, people believe their basic qualities, like their intelligence or talent, are simply fixed traits."

2. On the other hand, Dweck states, "In a growth mindset, people believe that their most basic abilities can be developed through dedication and hard work — brains and talent are just the starting point."

3. Pressure and fear are focus killers. Breathe, tell yourself you've got this, and know that it will be over. Arm yourself with positive self-talk and don't listen to what your anxiety tells you, even though the negative is so much easier to believe. Practice using a positive mantra.

4. Finish what you start even if you risk failure. There is always another time, another place, or another route to get where you want to be. Letting go of fear is emotionally freeing and liberates the soul.

5. A heightened sense of anxiety only increases one's fear of failure. Use Dweck's idea of a growth mindset and apply the formula of talent plus effort to get the best outcome.

Chapter 12
Self-Respect Is a Must

Arrogance is one of the character traits I most like to observe in other people. As a recruiter, I run into arrogant individuals on a regular basis. I love hearing people boast about how much money they are making and how they can't stop making money, or how the energy markets are working in their favor. All the while, the energy markets are in the toilet and companies are going out of business left and right. It seems to be a quality that comes with the territory. I've learned to look at it a different way.

Business development is one of my strong suits, or at least I thought it was. I invited a senior vice president of trading from a global energy company for coffee. I was diligently trying to recruit for this company, and he was the person I needed to get in with. He must have turned me down ten times before he finally agreed to meet me. His name was Mitch, and he was known for being a jerk and having an explosive personality. I did my homework and spoke to multiple colleagues in the industry about him. If I was to impress him — or at least not alienate him — I had to learn everything about him I could. The feedback I got was consistently negative. "He's a douche bag"; "I fucking hate him"; "I'd never work for that guy"; "He's a jerk." Every response I got was along the same lines.

I called Mitch at the office one day, still trying to get my meeting, and he happened to pick up. I was shocked and not prepared to talk to him. I'd fully expected his voicemail or his assistant. I stumbled over my words for a few seconds and then I asked him to give me thirty minutes of his time, tops. If he didn't like what I had to say, I would leave him alone. His manner was not very professional, but, to my surprise, he agreed to meet me. I confirmed the time and the place and told him I would be wearing a black pantsuit. His response was, "I don't care what you're wearing," and then he hung up on me.

I arrived twenty minutes early and secured a table. I waited and waited, but he wasn't showing up. Finally, after forty minutes, Mitch walked in. I leaped off my chair and walked over to shake his hand. He didn't smile and seemed agitated. I offered him a seat and asked the server to please bring a coffee. Mitch didn't waste any time. As soon as he sat down, he said, "You have thirty minutes. Go." His rude attitude was throwing me off, and I couldn't remember anything I wanted to tell him about why he should be working with my company. I just started babbling. His cellphone rang in the middle of our conversation, and Mitch did not bother with any of polite conventions like saying "Excuse me" — he simply got up, walked away, and answered the call. When he came back and sat down again, Mitch put his phone in his pocket, looked at his watch, and told me I had ten minutes and I'd better use it wisely. Never mind the fact that he'd just spent quite a few of my thirty minutes on the phone. I was unnerved by his arrogance and his obvious lack of interest in anything I had to say, and I struggled to get the conversation back on track. Why was he wasting my time and his? Why had he agreed to meet with me if he had no intention of listening or even pretending to care?

At this point I was quite rattled and struggled to regain my composure. My neck started to break out in hives as Mitch told me the meeting was a waste of time and he didn't see the value in what I brought to the table. Agitated and shocked, I apologized and told him I wanted to meet with him at another time, when we could have a more in-depth discussion. His response was so rude that it caught me off guard. He asked me not to contact him anymore, and he wouldn't even let me pay for the coffee he had barely touched, even though it was my meeting and therefore my responsibility. I put my hand out to thank him for his time, but he just turned and walked off. I was stunned. Why was he so obnoxious?

I sat back down for a few minutes to gather my thoughts. Our conversation was loud enough that other people around me had overheard Mitch's insults. I was so thrown off that I literally couldn't talk or look up; I just stared at the table and tapped my fingers on my coffee cup, trying to process the interaction. A gentleman sitting at the table next to me walked up and asked if I was okay. I said yes, but it was obvious I was not. The gentleman was a Vietnam veteran and was wearing a jacket with several patches on it. He told me he didn't like the way that guy was talking to me and he wanted to know if there was anything he could do for me.

Unfortunately, there was nothing this stranger could do to comfort me; I might have gotten a little satisfaction out of seeing him put Mitch in a chokehold, but I refrained from suggesting that. The stranger made me feel validated in some way — at least he had heard what I heard and had seen what I saw, uncomfortable as the interaction had been. I thanked him for his concern and acted like nothing was wrong. I then quickly got my check from the server and left the café. I drove home in silence, replaying Mitch's comments over and over in my head. I had blown the meeting, but I couldn't really figure out how or why. I'd barely spent any time talking to him. What could I have done differently?

The meeting with Mitch rattled me for days. I'd never had anyone do something like that. As a recruiter, I get told no frequently, but this wasn't just a no; it was a tongue-lashing.

Six months later, Mitch got fired, and the news spread like wildfire in the industry publications, as well as in electronic news feeds such as Reuters. The energy industry was buzzing with talk about how Mitch had lost an incredible amount of money for the company and wouldn't listen to his team of employees. People were glad to see Mitch get canned; he was not a well-liked person and was known for having a volatile personality and for publicly shaming his employees. The company was willing to put up with Mitch's attitude if he was making money; however, they should have had a "no asshole" policy in place. People like Mitch don't have a bad attitude because they've had a bad day; these types of people have the same attitude every single day and are destined to be fired at some point. As soon as I got wind of Mitch's involuntary departure, I called the company and offered to find his replacement, for free. The hiring manager was a friend of mine, and he knew what a jerk Mitch was, so he thought my offer was hilarious.

Looking back, I should have cancelled the meeting as soon as Mitch said he didn't care and hung up on me. He was profoundly disrespectful from the start, and I should have ended it at that very moment. Instead, I was so determined to get the account that I compromised my personal integrity. Mitch's arrogance and ego spoke volumes about his lack of character. Anyone who is that rude and unprofessional does not deserve your time, no matter how important the account.

Arrogance is a character flaw, a psychological shield used to cover up insecurities. It's a strategy intended to artificially inflate one's image in order to deflect from their weaknesses, failures, or incompetence and to establish superiority. It's an ugly interpersonal quality used to establish dominance and make others feel inferior and undeserving.

Be aware of such individuals and of their boastful behavior; they massage their own egos by putting down others just so they can parade their power. People like that will wreak havoc on you and your relationships; keep them at bay. It can be very educational to observe them. You start recognizing them faster and learning to walk away faster.

Key Points:

1. Arrogance is a sign of insecurity and self-doubt; people use it to deflect attention from the things they don't want you to see.

2. Don't allow arrogant people to fluster you; they will eventually be exposed for exactly what they are: insecure assholes!

3. Self-respect is non-negotiable. Be bold and walk away from disrespectful discussions, even if it means losing the relationship.

4. Arrogance is a character flaw — a psychological shield used to cover up insecurities. It's a strategy intended

to artificially inflate one's image in order to deflect from their weaknesses, failures, or incompetence and to establish superiority. Recognize it for what it is and don't tolerate it.

5. Be aware of such individuals and of their boastful behavior; they massage their own egos by putting down others just so they can parade their power. People like that will wreak havoc on you and your relationships; keep them at bay.

Chapter 13
Locus of Control — "It's Not My fault"

"In personality psychology, 'locus of control' refers to the extent to which individuals believe they can control events affecting them. A person's 'locus' is conceptualized as either internal (the person believes they can control their life) or external (meaning they believe their decisions and life are controlled by environmental factors which they cannot influence, or by chance or fate). Individuals with a strong internal locus of control believe events in their life derive primarily from their own actions: for example, when receiving exam results, people with an internal locus of control tend to praise or blame themselves and their abilities. People with a strong external locus of control tend to praise or blame external factors such as the teacher or the exam." — Wikipedia.com

My friend Kelley's ex-husband, Robert, is a great example of a person with an external locus of control. Before Robert and Kelley divorced, tension was already building up in their relationship, and there were a few events that escalated the disagreements between them. One of the most telling stories I've heard from Kelley is about a night when she was at home with the three children while Robert was out at a business dinner at Morton's, a steakhouse in Houston. Robert told Kelley the guys on his trading desk had performed really well and he wanted to take them out for a celebratory dinner. He wouldn't be long, he told her, maybe a couple of hours, and then he would be home to say goodnight to the kids.

Kelley went about her evening in the usual way: she gave the kids baths, fed them, read them a story, and got them ready for bed. Kelley was expecting Robert to be home by the children's bedtime, which was 8 p.m., but he wasn't. She kept them up later than usual, so that Robert would be able to see them before they went to bed. By 9 p.m. Kelley had not heard anything from Robert and was having a hard time keeping the children occupied. She called Robert's cellphone and got his voicemail, so she left a message saying she couldn't keep the kids up any longer and she was putting them to bed.

Kelley put the kids to sleep and retired to her bedroom to read and relax for the rest of the evening. By 11 p.m. she still hadn't heard from Robert, so she tried calling him again, but again his phone went straight to voicemail. Kelley was beginning to get a little worried, so she called Morton's too, and was told the restaurant was about to close shortly and all patrons had already left. Kelley tried to brush it off. Robert often stayed out longer than anticipated when he had business dinners or drinks with his friends. She assumed the team had moved somewhere else. By 1 a.m. Kelley was not only worried but also quite mad. She knew something wasn't right and began calling Robert's cellphone over and over, but his phone kept going straight to voicemail.

Kelley couldn't sleep, so she got out of bed and sat on the couch in the living room. At 1:45 a.m. Kelley heard Robert's car pull into the driveway. Anger took over at that point. She was fuming. She heard Robert shut the car door and turn on the alarm. Kelley waited for about ten minutes, but Robert still hadn't walked in the door. She decided she'd waited long enough, so she walked over and opened the door to find Robert standing naked with only his black dress socks on. He was holding his pants and button-down shirt balled up in his hands with a look of complete surprise on his face. Kelley quickly asked, "What are you doing?" Robert stumbled over his words. "I didn't want to wake you up by taking my clothes off in the house, so I thought it would be better if I took my clothes off outside and just throw them in the dry-cleaning basket."

Daggers shot out of Kelley's eyes. "I've been calling you for hours. Where have you been?" Robert explained that he was at a long dinner at Morton's and the team ended up having a productive conversation over some tasty Scotch. He said he was sorry that the dinner had lasted much longer than anticipated, but there was nothing he could do about it. Kelley told Robert about her phone call with Morton's. He swallowed uncomfortably and said, "That's not possible. I was there. Maybe you called the wrong Morton's."

Kelley could almost feel smoke rising from her ears. She knew Robert was lying and she suspected infidelity. "Hmm, that's interesting," she told him. "I called Morton's back and asked the manager if he knew what dinner party I was referring to, and he said yes, but the entire party had left the restaurant around nine thirty." Robert shrugged and said, "That's weird. I was there, babe, you can ask Ben." Ben was one of Robert's coworkers and his superior at the office. Ben had a reputation for being boring and straitlaced, and Kelley trusted him. By throwing his name out, Robert was trying to offer credibility to his story. Kelley stood there for a minute with her arms crossed and a look on her face that said, she knew it was a lie. She stepped forward and grabbed the balled-up clothes from

Robert's hands, enjoying his deer-in-headlights expression.

"Thank you for being so considerate," she said. "I'll take your clothes to the basket for you." Her tone was dripping with sinister sarcasm. Robert tried to grab the clothes back from Kelley, but she turned around quickly and walked toward the bedroom. He followed behind, completely naked apart from the black socks pulled up to the middle of his calves. He kept rambling. "It wasn't my fault — the guys wanted me to stay longer and I got caught up. I don't remember missing any calls, and by the time I realized my phone was off, I was pulling up in the driveway. Something must be wrong with my phone, I've been meaning to get it checked."

Kelley stopped, turned around to glare at Robert, and lifted his balled-up clothes to her face. She held his eyes and took a long, exaggerated sniff of his clothes. "Why do your clothes smell like perfume?" she asked. Robert denied it and called her crazy, but she knew he was lying. He had been caught philandering before, and his lying had become quite habitual. Kelley just walked into the bedroom, closed the door behind her, and locked it. Robert knew he was spending the night on the couch.

The next morning at 6 a.m. Kelley started getting the kids dressed. She didn't say a word to Robert, even though he continued to deny any wrongdoing and said the restaurant clearly made a mistake. None of this was his fault. Kelley ignored him. She got the kids dressed, ushered them into the car, and drove over to Ben's house. When she rang the doorbell, two giant poodles, one black and one white, rushed to the front door. It was winter, so the morning was

123

cold and dreary. Kelley was shivering as she rang the doorbell again and again.

Finally, Ben answered the door. His hair looked disheveled and he was yawning. He was surprised to see Kelley and asked if everything was okay. Kelley replied, "I apologize for waking you and your family up so early in the morning on a Saturday, but I have to ask you a question, and I need to know the answer as soon as possible. Were you with Robert last night at Morton's?" Ben said yes. Kelley asked him what time he left the restaurant. "About nine thirty, after we finished dinner," Ben said. "Why?"

Kelley felt like she had been punched in the stomach. She asked Ben if he went anywhere after the dinner, but he said he came straight home. Still confused, he asked Kelley what was going on. Kelley recounted the previous night's events. Ben looked surprised to hear Robert's story. He looked down at his feet and asked Kelley if she wanted to come in. Kelley declined. She just wanted to know what time Robert had left the restaurant.

Kelley arrived back at the house to find Robert pacing the hallway. Ben had called to tell him of Kelley's visit, so not only was Robert caught lying, but his colleague Ben now knew Robert's marriage was on the rocks.

Kelley took the kids upstairs and returned to the living room. Robert was furious about what she had done. She had not only embarrassed him in front of one of his colleagues, but she had possibly put his job at risk as well. Kelley was not interested in rehashing the rest of the story; she knew Robert was lying but didn't care to know what he had done after dinner. Plus, Robert himself told her to ask Ben if she doubted him.

Kelley's imagination was working overtime. Based on Robert's past behavior, she assumed he had ventured to an untoward venue after dinner. But was that all or was he actually cheating on her? She told Robert to go stay somewhere else for the time being, while she processed the situation.

Robert was enraged. He told Kelley she was overreacting as usual, but she stood her ground and told him to leave the house. Even while he was throwing clothes in a suitcase, Robert kept saying he'd done nothing wrong. None of it was his fault. Kelley did not engage with him. She just waited for the problem to be removed from the house, so she could process the situation and make a plan.

Just before he left, Robert yelled some things at Kelley: "This is your fault! Not only am I going to lose my job but now I'm going to lose my marriage. You need me, Kelley, you will never survive without me. I am your lifeline and you know it." With that, finally, he walked out and slammed the front door behind him.

Kelley didn't know what her next step should be. Part of her felt the marriage had run its course and was beyond repair. But part of her, the part that still held on to loyalty and commitment, wondered if she was giving up on the marriage too soon. Maybe they still had a chance to work things out.

Robert, a shameless manipulator, had once again gotten into Kelley's psyche and made her think she was the one at fault here. Had she made him so unhappy that she'd caused him to stray? Clearly, she was a terrible wife, or why else would he cheat on her and lie to her?

Kelley was internalizing the issue and magnifying her perceived inadequacies, whether they were real or not. Maybe it was her fault. Maybe the situation would not have escalated to this point if she hadn't been so quick to react.

Kelley was blaming herself for Robert's misdemeanors and transgressions. This line of thought was a spiral of self-sabotage.

Robert's pronounced external locus of control gave him all the reasons he needed to absolve himself of any responsibility for his own actions. He did not want to accept that he was in control and he had no intention of admitting to lying; he was too busy placing blame on Kelley. Robert's behavior was atrocious, and his default attitude was to insinuate that his failures and troubles were a function of somebody else's behavior. "It wasn't me, that's not my fault, you made me do it, you didn't listen, that's not what I said, you ran into me, you distracted me," etc. After so many excuses, Robert believed his own lies. Denial is a powerful thing.

Kelley is the flip side of the coin: she has an internal locus of control. In any situation, she believes she caused the outcome; it was her action of showing up on Ben's front door and telling him what happened that made her responsible if Robert lost his job. Kelley blamed herself, her attitude, and her reactive behavior for causing the problems.

Key Points:

1. A person with an internal locus of control blames their actions, behaviors, and life events on themselves.

2. A person with an external locus of control blames outside influences and forces for whatever happens to them in life.

3. People who take responsibility for their actions gain self-respect and have the power to change. Don't go overboard blaming yourself, like Kelley.

4. Character can be defined by knowing if a person has an internal or an external locus of control. If you constantly blame others for your own mistakes and failures, you have no room to grow as a person. Be accountable for your own actions.

5. Don't let people with an external locus of control manipulate you into internalizing the blame for their actions. Do not take responsibility for other people's behavior.

Chapter 14
Manipulative People

A man we will call James, someone I know well in real life, was married to a woman we will call Carrie. James and Carrie had been married for several years when their relationship began to unravel at lightning speed.

James and Carrie, both in their late twenties, met through a mutual friend at a dinner party in Houston and were attracted to each other from the moment they were first introduced. James was immediately infatuated with Carrie's appearance and said he knew from the minute he met her that she was the one. Carrie was a tall, raven-haired beauty with locks that cascaded down her back. She had big blue eyes with long eyelashes and a baby-like complexion. Carrie had a high school education and worked as an administrative assistant at a small telecommunications company. James graduated from one of the top business colleges in the United States with a degree in finance and was an equity trader at a global investment bank.

Carrie moved in with James practically overnight, and within six months they were engaged. James's mom, Sophia, lived in Dallas and did not come to Houston often, but she scheduled a time to come and meet James and Carrie for lunch. Unfortunately, the day they were supposed to meet, Carrie didn't feel well. She told James to go by himself, and she would meet Sophia next time she was in town. James agreed, and went by himself. Sophia expressed her disappointment that Carrie couldn't make it. She wondered if Carrie was deliberately avoiding her but gave her the benefit of the doubt.

Two weeks later, Sophia came back to Houston again. She arranged to meet Carrie and James for lunch at a beautiful French café with a fantastic reputation. Sophia ordered a bottle of Veuve Clicquot and told the waiter it was a special occasion: She was about to meet her soon-to-be daughter-in-law.

Carrie and James showed up to the café twenty minutes late for lunch, which was unusual for James. However, Sophia shrugged off the inconvenience and told Carrie how excited she was to finally meet her. She offered Carrie a seat next her and started to pour her a glass of champagne for a toast. Carrie quickly put her hand over her glass and told Sophia she didn't drink alcohol and would prefer sparkling water instead. Sophia didn't skip a beat and immediately asked the waiter for a glass of sparkling water. Sophia raised her glass, made a toast to James and Carrie, and told both how happy she was they had found each other. As a gift, Sophia told Carrie she would pay for a highly recommended wedding coordinator to make sure Carrie would have the perfect wedding. Carrie politely smiled and thanked Sophia. Moments later, as Sophia was asking Carrie questions about her family, Carrie abruptly excused herself from the table, saying she had to go to the ladies' room. When she came back to the table, Carrie sweetly said that she was so sorry, but she was not going to be able to stay long; her sister was in town and needed help finding a dress for an event. Sophia was slightly taken aback at this turn of events but handled the situation gracefully and told Carrie what a pleasure it had been to meet her. James looked uncomfortable and uneasy.

Carrie left, and Sophia quickly turned to James and started asking him about Carrie 's behavior. Why was she so evasive? Why couldn't she stay for lunch with her soon-to-be mother-in-law? Sophia thought Carrie was acting odd — she had already bailed on lunch once, and now she had to leave early to help her sister? James tried to smooth the situation over and assured Sophia that Carrie was a nice girl and that Sophia was simply overreacting.

Carrie and Sophia did not have much interaction throughout the wedding planning process, until Sophia received a call from the wedding coordinator. Because Carrie did not like the centerpieces the coordinator had picked for the rehearsal dinner, she had fired her on the spot. Sophia was shocked and quickly called James to find out what was going on. James explained that Carrie did not feel the wedding coordinator was compatible with her taste and what she envisioned the wedding to be. Sophia saw this as another red flag, but James assured her everything was fine.

Sophia desperately wanted to get along with Carrie, but somehow, they seemed to have gotten off on the wrong foot. James was Sophia's only child, and she wanted to be involved in his life. Sophia made several attempts to get to know Carrie; she asked Carrie out for lunch, tried to ingratiate herself by gushing over how beautiful Carrie was, but nothing seemed to bring Sophia closer. Carrie was taking all of James's time, and Sophia began noticing a change in his behavior. He was short with Sophia and wasn't available to meet her for lunch or talk about the wedding plans. Sophia felt distanced from both of them and wrestled with the thought of bringing up her feelings to James. She sensed, with every fiber of her being, that Carrie was not the right girl for James, but she kept her feelings to herself. Before Carrie came along, James had been in a ten-year relationship with his high school girlfriend, whom Sophia thought very well of. However, with Carrie, something wasn't right.

Carrie and James got married after a year of dating, and Carrie quickly became pregnant with their first child, Chloe. A year later they had their second child, Justin, and the following year they had their third, Thomas. James was in the prime of his career and working furiously to climb the corporate ladder. When he was twenty-nine, James received a huge bonus of $1.2 million. It was more money than he could have imagined he would ever make. Although from the outside James appeared to be doing well, something was missing. The next year, at age thirty, he received an even larger bonus of $1.8 million. James was at the top of his game; he had a beautiful wife, three healthy children, and a lucrative career. Although his job required him to move his family around the U.S. and Europe in order to continue getting promoted, he always consulted Carrie. She didn't like to stay in one place very long, so she was on board with every move. Carrie and James lived in beautiful homes all over the world, including in Texas, Oklahoma, New York, and France. They had a summer home in Florida, and they took lavish family vacations to Sardinia, Monte Carlo, England, the Bahamas, and many more.

One afternoon, James came home from work to find Carrie beaming in excitement. She had just purchased $300,000 worth of new furnishings for their 6,500-square-foot home in Chicago. James was shocked and could barely utter a word. In the past few months they had somehow gone from being very comfortable financially to living paycheck to paycheck. Before meeting Carrie, James had been a financially responsible individual with disciplined spending habits, but Carrie 's expensive tastes and lavish lifestyle had slowly pushed them over the edge. Now this latest of Carrie's unplanned-for extravagances was going to set them back even more.

James was beginning to feel burned out; he was the sole breadwinner, and he didn't know how he could maintain their high-end lifestyle and Carrie's spending habits. He began showing outward signs of distress, such as weight gain, rosacea on his cheeks, and eczema on his hands. Their financial situation was worsening. James wasn't sleeping very well and was in a state of constant worry. Oftentimes, he took sleeping pills so he would not stay up all night worrying about the future. The money was going out faster than it was coming in, and he had no guarantee what his paycheck would be like next year.

From a personality perspective, James and Carrie were quite different. Carrie had a confident personality and carried herself with an air of entitlement. She was often described as intelligent but a know-it-all. She didn't have many friends except for her family members, her hairstylist, and the lady who did her nails. James was quiet, with a laid-back disposition. He was well liked, intelligent, and well spoken, and he had lots of longtime friends. He was often described by his friends and coworkers as a great guy. James did not come off as the warmest person in the world when you first met him, but after a few minutes of conversing with him, you began to not only like him, you trusted and respected him.

Carrie had been married once before, when she was eighteen; she claimed it was a marriage her parents pushed her to go through with. By the time she was twenty-one, she had already filed for bankruptcy and was divorced, but at least back then she did not have children to worry about. She was reckless with her finances and had no self-control over her spending; more importantly, she just did not care what her financial situation was. If she had access to money, she spent it without a worry in the world. A few years after her divorce, Carrie met James, and they were married right after her twenty-fifth birthday.

James had never married, but he and his high school girlfriend were together for ten years. James remained friends with her and even became friends with her husband when she got married. He had good morals, good values, and showed a great respect toward women.

By the time Carrie and James had their third child, Thomas, their marriage was beginning to take a turn for the worse. James wasn't making as much money, and the excitement of moving from place to place for his career had faded. Carrie, recently obsessed with health and fitness, spent an inordinate amount of time at the gym every day — two to six hours. She became obsessed with her personal appearance. She would have a sitter watch the kids while she went to the gym in the mornings, and, when James came home in the evenings, Carrie would hand the children over to him and head out the door to the gym for another workout session. She worked on her body relentlessly, until James began to suspect her dedication to the gym might be more than just a healthy addiction. He found it odd that Carrie was working out twice daily and decided to look into her behavior.

One day while James was backing Carrie's car out of the driveway, James found a hotel keycard in the middle console of her car. When he confronted Carrie, she denied having any knowledge of the keycard and claimed somebody must have put the keycard there by mistake. James was furious; he knew she was lying, but Carrie continued to deny any wrongdoing and accused James of being a crazy jealous husband.

James began looking at Carrie 's phone records, credit card statements, and tollbooth receipts, which unveiled a pattern of betrayal that had been going on for months. He knew she was having an affair but was unsure whether it was with one person or several. James suspected she was having an affair with her personal trainer but had no real proof until now. Through tollbooth receipts he was able to verify that Carrie was not actually going to the gym, which was just ten minutes away from the house. Carrie's phone records revealed that she had been consistently calling and receiving calls from one particular number, and there was a large amount of data used as well.

Carrie adamantly denied the claims and accused James of making a mountain out of a molehill. She was so firm in her denial that James was starting to doubt his own sanity. Was he really overreacting? Was he being jealous and unreasonable? But he couldn't ignore the hard evidence, which told a much different story from what Carrie wanted him to believe. She had a ton of explanation for the calls and tollbooth receipts: *She had to go through the tollbooths on the other side of town, so she could get vitamins and weightlifting gear before heading back to the gym, but she didn't do it every time. The tollbooths were not always accurate and there must have been a mistake with the timing. She wasn't the one driving the car that night* (although who else could it have been?). *She couldn't remember every single time she went through the tollbooth. The personal trainer was just a friend, nothing more. They called each other frequently to strategize about fitness competitions.* The list went on and on. She would not concede that she had done anything out of the ordinary.

But James had identified a pattern in Carrie's behavior, and he knew she was lying, despite all the evidence he presented to her. Her lies didn't make any sense.

A couple of weeks after confronting Carrie about the hotel keycard in her car, the unreasonable number of workouts, and the tollbooth receipts, James went on a business trip to South America. He was depressed and conflicted about the state of his marriage. The relationship had fallen apart very quickly from out of nowhere, and James had no idea how to go about repairing it.

When he returned, he was mentally and emotionally drained. As soon as he walked in the door, he saw a set of legal documents waiting for him on a table in the entryway. Carrie hadn't wasted any time after their confrontation; she had filed for divorce while James was away. James pleaded with Carrie to change her mind, but it was as if he was talking to a complete stranger; she was cold, calculating, and ruthless. Carrie was ready to move on, and she wanted to do it like she did everything else — as quickly as possible.

Shortly after Carrie filed for divorce, James lost his job as a trader at a hedge fund he had been working at for only six weeks. James had switched jobs for an opportunity to make more money, but the fund put on a trading position that went against the market, and the company ended up having to file for bankruptcy. James and Carrie were in real financial trouble. They had $200,000 in credit card debt, a beach house in foreclosure, and no expendable cash to speak of.

The divorce was fifteen months of hell — that's how long it took from the time Carrie filed for divorce to the time it was granted. James had to liquidate his assets and drain his 401(k) to pay for the divorce, which ended up costing hundreds of thousands of dollars. Carrie filed injunction after injunction after injunction, which were quite expensive, to get the outcome she wanted. Carrie was awarded $7,000 per month in child support and the court granted her permission to move the children to Los Angeles, where she would be able to be by her family. James was left broke, beaten down, and alone.

The most telling part of Carrie's lying was her request to have a statement in the divorce decree saying she did not have an extramarital affair and that James was prohibited from saying anything about Carrie being unfaithful to the children. James didn't have to agree to the statement, however, at this point, it didn't matter. He just wanted to be done with her. Plus, her statement was a really just a big admission of guilt.

People like Carrie should come with giant red blinking signs on top of their heads that read: P A R A S I T E. From the moment James got involved with her, Carrie moved quickly to isolate him from his friends and family, deplete him of his resources, and then move on. Only James's mom, Sophia, had instantly picked up on Carrie's manipulative behavior, and, once Carrie knew Sophia had figured her out, Carrie couldn't get away from her fast enough.

Keep your distance from manipulative people; their sole goal is to look for your weakness and exploit it. Anyone who has your best interests at heart will not isolate you from your friends and family, consistently violate your boundaries, psychologically torture you, or demand unreasonable requests from you. Keep your power, set boundaries, and say no if a request seems unreasonable. Lastly, don't be afraid to turn the tables on the manipulator by asking probing question that expose the nature of the ruse. "Does this sound like a good plan to you?" "Is this a fair trade in your mind?" "If I asked you to do this exact request for me, would you?" "Is this something you have done yourself?" Anyone with a smidge of self-awareness will back down.

Key Points:

1. Beware of people who do not have friends other than the people who perform a service for them; i.e. nail technician, hair stylist, house cleaner, etc.

2. Manipulators will try to isolate you from people they feel will influence your thinking.

3. People who can easily walk away from a meaningful relationship as if it were an old newspaper have no regard for your well-being; don't walk away from them, RUN away.

4. Keep your distance from manipulative people. Their sole goal is to look for your weakness and exploit it.

5. If all else fails, the best way to get a manipulative person to back down is to ask probing questions to expose their ruse.

Chapter 15
Parasitic Lifestyle

In the previous chapter, you were introduced to Carrie and James. In this chapter, we will focus on Carrie and take a deeper look into her behavior and personality traits. The importance of doing this is to help you recognize when you are dealing with a person you need to get away from immediately. The only tool to use with these people is to RUN; all other tools are worthless.

Parasites suck. Literally — they suck. From *New Oxford American Dictionary:* "A parasite is any organism that lives and feeds off of another organism (its host) and benefits by deriving nutrients at the host's expense." Of course, I'm using the term "parasite" to refer to a person who takes advantage of others and exploits them without giving anything in return, but it's useful to remember the literal definition as well. It helps to remind us what we're really up against when we meet such people.

Carrie is/was a parasite. She fed off James, drained him financially and emotionally until he had nothing, and then, when he dared to confront her about her behavior, she dumped him to move on to a new host with a lot more money.

Carrie had a high school education and no career to speak of other than living a parasitic life off of men. She had no true friends, moved around frequently, and always left a trail of destruction. People who fell prey to her charms were left penniless and devastated.

A few years after James and Carrie divorced, she moved to Denver, Colorado. She bought a house with her settlement money and soon began dating a man more than twenty years her senior. With a net worth in the $50 million range, he was a hell of a catch. Carrie honed in with lightning speed, and within a year she was engaged to Mr. Millionaire.

Mr. Millionaire was a fifty-six-year-old shrewd businessman who built a life insurance business worth millions. Mr. Millionaire was even recognized by *Forbes* magazine for being one of the wealthiest CEOs in the United States. He was a pretty big deal. Mr. Millionaire had been married once before, for twenty years, and he had five children, all grown up by the time he met Carrie.

I am unsure how exactly Carrie was able to get in front of Mr. Millionaire, but if I had to guess, I would say she looked through *Forbes*'s list and then did her research from there. She came in, as Mylie Cyrus would say, like a wrecking ball, and somehow managed to win Mr. Millionaire over. The courtship was a six-month whirlwind of traveling around the world, escorting Mr. Millionaire on his many business trips.

Carrie had several nannies for the children throughout the years. She usually had a live-in nanny, so she could travel on short notice and be gone for long periods of time. Of course, once a nanny got too close to her children, jealousy reared its ugly head, and Carrie would come up with a reason to fire her. Carrie was not going to be upstaged. She would accuse the nannies of stealing a piece of jewelry or just tell them they were not meeting her expectations and their services were no longer needed. Carrie went through nannies as if they were newspapers; she simply tossed them aside like yesterday's news.

Once Carrie and Mr. Millionaire became engaged, Carrie instructed the children that they were to call him "Dad" from that point on. Although they were uncomfortable with this, Carrie would not allow them to call him anything else. Mr. Millionaire, Carrie, and her three children moved into a beautiful home on top of a mountain in Denver, Colorado. The mansion had five bedrooms, a custom-made theater room, a gym, a gated winding driveway, three garages, a porte-cochère, an industrial-size kitchen, and a pond in front of the house with two real swans floating about. There were several ornate balconies with a view of the spectacular snow-covered mountains. The mansion was breathtaking. Carrie was extremely pleased with herself; in her mind, she had finally arrived.

Mr. Millionaire spared no expense when it came to Carrie and her children. All three of the children were enrolled in an exclusive private school that cost upwards of $25,000 per year, per student. They had a daytime nanny to watch the children while Carrie was working out and getting her hair done, and a nighttime nanny who could sleep over if Carrie and Mr. Millionaire needed to go out for dinner or out of town for the evening. Mr. Millionaire also bought Carrie a $350,000 black convertible Rolls Royce, and a $425,000 red Lamborghini for himself.

Carrie proclaimed herself to be a personal trainer and life coach, although she had no certifications to do either (huge red flag). She did spend a lot of time at the gym while Mr. Millionaire was working and traveling. When she was not at the gym or escorting Mr. Millionaire on his private plane to business dinners in New York, she was getting hair extensions and highlights, getting facials, tanning, and getting her nails done. Mr. Millionaire traveled frequently, which meant that Carrie had a lot of free time on her hands. She would have her friends from the gym come over to her home gym, where they would practice dance routines and work out. Amongst these gym friends was Carrie's personal trainer, Alan, who would frequently train with her at her house when Mr. Millionaire was out of town.

After they'd been married for six months, Mr. Millionaire began suspecting that Carrie was having an affair. She had become more secretive, and sometimes when he asked her about her friends and what she'd been up to, he got the impression that she was not telling him the whole story. Mr. Millionaire was determined to find out the truth, so he asked one of the IT guys at his office to hack into his wife's email. When the employee refused, Mr. Millionaire fired him. Weeks later, the employee ended up filing a lawsuit against Mr. Millionaire for asking him to do something that was illegal and then firing him when he refused. It was an embarrassing moment for Mr. Millionaire; however, he had a strong suspicion that his young, hot wife was having an affair, and he wanted proof. He ended up settling the lawsuit for an undisclosed amount.

I'm not sure if Mr. Millionaire was eventually able to get proof of Carrie's infidelity, but they were divorced within a year from the day they got married. With the scandal about him tampering with her email, she had him in a corner, and Mr. Millionaire quickly made a $2 million settlement to make her go away. Carrie moved the three children into another home, right down the street from Mr. Millionaire, for six months while she plotted her next move, which was to Miami, Florida. It was time to look for another host.

Carrie moved to Miami, Florida, and paid cash for a $1.1 million home in a posh gated community. Alan, her personal trainer, who was now her boyfriend, had moved to Seattle, but he would come and stay with Carrie for months a time. They got to work spending the money from Carrie's divorce settlement. They had a pool put in her new home. They bought a boat, a red Corvette, a fully furnished rental property on the beach, and a condo in the Caribbean. And they took lots of lavish trips. Carrie also had a new full-time nanny in exchange for room and board.

Carrie was a social media queen, with an impressive 100,000 followers; she plastered her face and body on any and every outlet she could think of. With the money from her divorce settlement, Carrie self-published a book on fitness — mostly a picture book of her rock-hard body — and launched a nutrition bar with a picture of her awesome self on the packaging. Carrie marketed herself as a divorced mother of three who was once overworked and overweight until she invented this magical nutrition bar that changed her life. She had never been overweight in the least, and in her picture book she had only one picture of her "fat" self, from when she was eight months pregnant. Conveniently, she forgot to mention this fact in the caption of the photo.

Carrie's business ventures didn't succeed. Her nutrition bar did not sell, and she ended up with boxes of expired bars stacked in her garage. The book didn't sell either, but both products lent Carrie some perceived credibility as an entrepreneur and gave her something to put on her business card. Carrie was a master at spinning stories, and that is exactly what she did. She reframed her numerous moves, nannies, bankruptcy, and divorces to sound like learning experiences that made her the successful person she had become. What utter poppycock.

For a while, life was going pretty well for Carrie, until she once again started running low on money and got bored; she needed to find another host to feed on. When the housing market began to decline, Carrie started losing money on some of her investments, so she began liquidating her assets. She put her house and rental property on the market, sold the boat and the Corvette, and moved into a smaller rental property. By this point, Carrie and Alan had rifled through most of the money. When Alan got wind of how little was left, he hopped on the first plane back to Seattle. All the while Carrie was looking for a new victim for her parasitic scam.

Carrie decided to move to Baltimore, Maryland where her parents lived. She needed to generate some goodwill with her family, so she could restore her reputation and appear to be more stable than she was. Everything she did was calculated. Carrie bought a huge house on the same street where her parents lived, and they were thrilled. She began making appearances with her children at church and going over to her parents' house for Sunday dinners. She even hired a new nanny from the church, which helped to secure her new wholesome image, which in turn pleased her parents. After she'd put in some dedicated time and was starting to see people reacting to her differently, Carrie began traveling weekly to Scottsdale, Arizona, where she would stay for three to five days at a time. She told her parents she was meeting with investors to fund her business ventures, so she could get her brand out in the market.

After a year in Baltimore Maryland, Carrie sold her house and moved into a rental property close to Scottsdale, Arizona, one of the most expensive areas in the United States: Her rent was $8,000 per month, but Carrie had a breathtaking view of the desert, mountains, and sunsets.

She enrolled the kids in the local public schools and hired a new nanny to shuttle them around town.

Carrie instantly started having an affair with a billionaire entrepreneur in his mid-fifties who was married and had two young children. He left his wife of fifteen years shortly thereafter, and it was known throughout Scottsdale that the reason for the separation was Carrie. Needless to say, the billionaire's divorce was not amicable. The Scottsdale community was abuzz with gossip. "The wives of Scottsdale," as they were known, put their noses in the air and refused to socialize with Carrie. They had no room in their circle for a husband-stealing trollop with a questionable background. This did not seem to bother Carrie, though. She went about her business and ignored the women in the neighborhood. By this point, Carrie was close to forty, which was close to the average age in this community of wealthy individuals.

The billionaire had an impressive education and had made his billions in the information technology and software markets. He had a $10 million home in New Jersey, a home in Hawaii, private planes, and much more. Carrie had found her new host. Six months after Carrie arrived in Scottsdale, she and the billionaire got engaged and moved into a $25 million home. Carrie was pushing forward like fire through a field.

Carrie's own business endeavors were not nearly successful enough to afford her a luxury living. She wasn't making any money off her nutrition bar and her book, so it was imperative that she use other people's money to maintain the Hollywood lifestyle she had grown accustomed to. Carrie traveled on private planes, lived in beautiful mansions, drove expensive cars, and socialized with an elite philanthropic society. She still had the $7,000 per month from James for child support — not chump change by any means. Carrie always found a way to justify more expenses for the children and drain James financially. She lived a parasitic lifestyle, moving from person to person and sucking each of them dry until they were financially ruined.

How did these well-educated, successful, savvy individuals fall for someone like Carrie? Aside from the fact that she was a psychopath, which meant she was an excellent manipulator, Carrie presented herself to the outside world as a successful entrepreneur. With pictures of her super-fit body featured prominently on her multiple websites and on her fitness book, she appeared legitimate. However, she was not really successful — unless you count feeding off of and draining someone else financially as a success. Anyone who bothered to look a bit closer would have found out that she did not have any degrees or certifications that qualified her to be a life coach or fitness trainer. Carrie claimed in her book to have trained with professional athletes, but she hadn't. It was a blanket claim too general to verify. This was one of several vague statements in her book that served to establish her legitimacy and lend her credibility as a professional fitness coach. Carrie had never taught a fitness class or counseled someone on nutrition; her claims were completely fabricated.

Through the years, because of her extravagant lifestyle and her lack of stable income, Carrie frequently found herself in debt up to her eyeballs. This is also why she didn't stay in one place for very long. Once she suspected that people were beginning to catch onto her scam and figure out she wasn't what she proclaimed to be, Carrie would quickly move and start over in a new place, telling a new set of stories to a new set of people.

Within a five-year span, Carrie had moved to five different states and fifteen different houses, and her children had been to six different schools. Unless you are in the military, that's a staggering number of moves. As a result, Carrie's children did not have any friends except for each other, and they struggled in school. The lack of stability and the constant change had greatly affected them. Frankly, they were a mess.

Carrie left a path of destruction everywhere she went. She was estranged from her siblings and she didn't have any true friends; all she had was admirers on social media, people who liked the photos she posted on Facebook and on her websites and who believed the stories about her success. Carrie didn't form any attachments either; anyone and anything was expendable to her. She was quick to sell her houses, furniture, and cars, and to cut relationships. Nothing held any lasting value to Carrie; everything and everyone were but a variable in a temporary transaction.

Hare's psychopathy checklist is a diagnostic test that measures a person's psychopathic qualities — such as superficial charm, pathological lying, lack of empathy, and many more.

Below are the traits on Hare's psychopathy checklist, with Carrie's traits shown in italics. The only traits that can't be verified are early childhood behavior and juvenile delinquency. But even without them, Carrie scored unbelievably high on the checklist. It's helpful to keep these characteristics in mind if you come across manipulative people. If they, like Carrie, display many of the traits below and exhibit similar behaviors, then you know you need to save yourself as soon as possible.

- *glib and superficial charm*
- *grandiose (exaggeratedly high) estimation of self*
- *need for stimulation*
- *pathological lying*
- *cunning and manipulativeness*
- *lack of remorse or guilt*
- *shallow affect (superficial emotional responsiveness)*
- *callousness and lack of empathy*
- *parasitic lifestyle*
- *poor behavioral controls*
- *sexual promiscuity*
- early behavior problems
- *lack of realistic long-term goals*
- *impulsivity*
- *irresponsibility*
- *failure to accept responsibility for own actions*
- *many short-term marital relationships*
- juvenile delinquency
- revocation of conditional release
- *criminal versatility*

Key Points:

1. "A parasite is any organism that lives and feeds off of another organism (its host) and benefits by deriving nutrients at the host's expense."

2. Be cautious around people who move in quickly and separate you from outside influences like friends and family.

3. Question individuals who claim to be experts but have no verifiable credentials.

4. People who don't stay in one place for very long should raise a red flag; there is a reason they keep moving.

5. Reference Hare's psychopathy checklist for qualities like superficial charm, pathological lying, lack of empathy, lake of conscience, sexual promiscuity, parasitic lifestyle, and others.

Chapter 16
Remaining Aloof

When someone is aloof, they are calm, reserved, and keep a safe distance. By remaining aloof, you leave a little bit of mystery about your disposition, and you don't show your cards. People will have trouble figuring you out, which protects you — otherwise, if people can read you like a book, they have power over you. To be aloof does not mean you have to be emotionally unavailable. The point is that there are times when remaining aloof can work to your benefit. Save your openness for close friends and family and maintain distance with others in order to protect yourself. Being aloof can have advantages in new relationships, legal battles, professional relationships, and business dealings in general.

While going through a divorce with my now ex-husband, I found myself in an unfamiliar emotional darkness. The toll the divorce took on my emotions was tremendous; I hope to never go to that mental place again. There were physical effects too. My skin began to break out in red puss filled bumps and red patches that, no matter what I did, I couldn't get under control. I was trying every face cleanser on the market, but, day after day, I would wake up to a whole new set of little friends clustered on my chin and jawline. It was horrible. I didn't want to leave the house, I just wanted to hide until it cleared up.

After a few months of consistent breakouts, I went to a dermatologist, where I discovered that I had adult acne. I had never had acne before, nor has anyone in my family, so I was unsure what could have caused such a dramatic shift in my skin. The dermatologist prescribed a few topical treatments and skin peels, but nothing worked. She then tried an antibiotic. As luck would have it, I was allergic to it, and my body broke out in large hives that itched like crazy. I was miserable. Finally, as a last resort, my dermatologist prescribed a very powerful drug called Accutane which is used to treat severe cystic acne. Accutane is a highly controversial drug that was originally meant as a chemotherapy drug but has become known for treating acne that is not responsive to antibiotics. The side effects of Accutane are very serious and include Crohn's disease, liver disease, suicide, birth defects, red cracked lips, headaches, bloody noses, and many more. I was terrified, but I couldn't hide forever, and I didn't want to show my face in public looking like a monster.

In order to take Accutane, I had to commit to an eight-month regimen of monthly doctor visits to get my blood drawn, take monthly pregnancy tests, be on two forms of birth control, and register with the I-Pledge Program, which was a computer-based test required from pharmacies, doctors, and patients and is intended to reinforce everyone's understanding of the dangers of the medicine. This time-consuming process is medically and contractually mandatory due to the severe side effects. Once I had completed all the above tasks each month, the doctor would write me a thirty-day prescription. The process felt like getting your driver's license, car inspection, and registration renewed every month for eight consecutive months. It was grueling, but I didn't care; I just wanted it to work.

After a few months on Accutane, I was beginning to see my skin clear up. I was so excited that finally something was working, and I was getting some relief. It took six months of dry chapped lips, red, burned-looking skin, bloody noses, and headaches for the acne to be almost completely gone. My dermatologist was very pleased with the way my body responded to the medicine and kept me on it for two more months, to make sure the acne was completely cleared up. On my last visit to the dermatologist, I asked her what she thought had caused my skin to break out with such severe acne, and her answer was surprising to me. She explained some of the more common reasons, including hormone changes due to having babies, genetics, and bacteria; however, she said stress was a big factor in acne flare-ups. My body's response to the stress of the divorce caused me to produce hormones that stimulated the oil glands and hair follicles in my skin, which led to the acne. My problem wasn't just a one-time flare-up of acne; it was an ongoing problem that was kick-started by the divorce. I was under constant stress and my body was manifesting it from the inside out.

Going through the divorce was significantly more draining than I could have imagined. Mentally, I believed that I couldn't survive on my own; I wasn't smart enough, I would fail, and my children were going to be emotionally traumatized. I doubted myself in every way. I didn't know how to start over, or how to be a single mom, or how to financially make ends meet. I was on a roller coaster of emotions, paralyzed with fear and wondering if I was making the right choice. The upside — I lost twenty pounds and I could finally fit into my swankalishious clothes. The downside — I was an emotional basket case. I felt weak and scared. The divorce not only depleted me emotionally and financially, it completely crippled me mentally. I would become highly reactive and angry when I heard worthless threats to obtain custody of the children or that my house would be foreclosed. I was angry, scared, and depressed, but I kept moving forward. The one thing I knew in my heart was that as long as I had my children, I didn't care if I lost my house or my belongings. It was, without a doubt, time to go.

My anger and defensiveness delighted my ex; in fact, he went to great lengths to antagonize me as much as possible, so he could sit back, laugh, and say, "Look how crazy you're acting. What is wrong with you?" His response frustrated me even more, to the point where I would slam the door in his face or make fun of his physical shortcomings. I wanted to wound him with my words, but that only fed into his plan to anger me even more. When I allowed him to get under my skin — when I yelled and called him insulting names — I knew I had lost the argument. I basically handed him the trophy at that point. It was time for me to get a new strategy and a better game plan. Finally, I was able to recognize his pattern of purposely provoking me to react, to the point where every encounter escalated, so I decided to do the opposite; I became aloof.

After nine years of marriage, our divorce became finalized; I felt like a boulder had been lifted off my shoulders. I started crying as I walked out of the courthouse to the parking garage across the street, but I couldn't figure out exactly why I was crying. Maybe it was because it was the end of the marriage, or perhaps it was the new beginning that now felt overwhelming. It was as if the rain clouds had lifted and the sun was coming out to shine right on my face.

After the divorce, the same issues continued with my ex but in a more detached way. I was living in the same house my ex and I had previously lived in and took over the mortgage payments. Although both our names were on the mortgage loan, I was granted sole ownership of the house in the divorce decree. My ex wanted his name off the mortgage, so he called me demanding that I refinance the house under my name only, which normally wouldn't be unreasonable. But I calmly explained that I was unable to do that due to my credit score being annihilated from the divorce. He became very angry and started lashing out with mean comments, telling me I was selfish and that I needed to find a way to make it happen. My ex had no control over whether or not his name was on the mortgage. It didn't affect him if he wanted to buy a house or prohibit him from getting a future loan; he was just being a bully and doing his best to inconvenience me as much as possible. Although I was the one who wanted the divorce, it was with good reason, so there was no need for bitterness. I tried to remind myself of that during the phone call. As I had planned, I remained aloof. After the second insult, I calmly told him I was unable to help, and he would need to take the issue up with the mortgage company. He began insulting me with rude and mean comments, at which point I ended the call. Two seconds later he called me back, but there was no reason for me to answer; he'd used up all my patience.

Two years after the divorce, I met and married my current husband, John. My ex tried his best to get to know John by initiating conversation with him or making a comment about an NFL game at the kids' football games, but John remained uninterested and aloof. He was always cordial but distant. My ex's old bag of tricks wasn't working on John — there was no satisfaction in playing a game with an aloof opponent. John is a natural when it comes to aloofness; he can ignore you like you're not even there.

On one occasion, me ex become jealous when he heard that John and I were taking the children to Disney World. We had planned a weeklong trip with John's three children, my three children, my mother-in-law, and my parents to stay in a twelve-person condo in the heart of the Animal Kingdom. The kids were so excited, they couldn't stop talking about all the different activities we had planned; they told everyone about the trip, including my ex. It didn't take long before I got a call from him about getting his name off the mortgage loan and threatening legal action if I did not accommodate his demands. I remained aloof, gave the conversation a limit of one insult, and promptly ended the call after that insult. I settled on this strategy through a process of trial and error, after many disagreements, not only with my ex but with other people in my personal and professional life. The strategy protected me from getting caught up in unnecessary drama.

Being aloof in business has served me well, especially when dealing with a boss who is a micromanager or a candidate who finds something wrong with every company they work for. When I encounter a power-hungry individual, whose only ambition is to achieve dominance to boost their own ego, I simply remain aloof and keep a safe psychological distance. This method helps me maintain a calm exterior and sends a message that I will not get caught up in emotional turmoil.

Learning to manage yourself in a conflict takes strategy and practice. Knowing your own triggers and staying on top of your hot buttons will keep you from jumping into the ring of chaos. Avoid the emotional trauma of a heated argument by becoming a strategic thinker with a plan.

The psychology behind being aloof is to remain neutral in a hostile situation so you do not reveal too much information. This tool has its advantages in social groups, business, dating, family events, and more. Aloofness is attractive, which means aloof people have the most power in social groups. Aloof behavior intrigues people; if you withhold something from them, it whets their curiosity and they want to know more about you. You present them with a puzzle they want to solve. The key is to give people the intrigue but never the satisfaction.

But being aloof can be a fine line to walk. You do not want to seem rude or uninterested, but at the same time you don't want to get pulled into other people's problems. You want to listen with compassion, offer your support, and then pull back. People may not like this, but it's smart to keep your emotions private, keep your coworkers at arm's length, and date with interest but maintain your distance, at least in the beginning.

I have candidates who will court me with gifts and praise in an effort to get me to commit my time solely to finding them a new job. I have received event invites, calls, unsolicited compliments, jewelry, candy, gift baskets, and wine; occasionally I've even come across candidates who've wanted to share their emotional woes with me to gain my attention, but I maintain aloofness for this very reason. Once I commit, I no longer have a safe distance. Although this may sound shallow, it's not. My interest in other people's affairs is legitimate, very legitimate, but remains on a surface level. It's a good practice for everyone to follow. Be cautious and don't allow anyone to put you under obligation. It's okay to have a sense of mystery about you, but, more importantly, it's okay to have boundaries so you can avoid getting sucked into unnecessary problems.

There is a fine line between being aloof and being uninterested; you don't want to appear as if you don't care, which can be off-putting. You want to maintain just the right level of aloofness, so it makes people curious and they want to know more about you; they will want to know what you think about the new office policy or which way you are leaning on the controversial debates. Give them just enough information but not too much. You still care, but you care about yourself more. People like a challenge, but not a constant challenge. You may even accept a small gift from a candidate, like a $10 bottle of wine, but don't trade your mental and emotional peace for that gift. Protect yourself above all and remember that making a commitment to someone just because you feel indebted to them is never advantageous to your position.

Key Points:

1. By remaining aloof in difficult situations, you create a distance from your opponent and protect yourself.

2. There are certain situations in which being aloof can play to your advantage — for example, in business negotiations or when arguing with an ex-partner. However, do not use aloofness in an emergency or in a situation that requires your immediate attention.

3. In personal as well as in business dealings, losing your temper will not get you anywhere — all it does is show a lack of emotional control. Practice remaining aloof instead.

4. Once character assassinations and insults enter a conversation, it is no longer a productive dialogue and should be ended immediately.

5. When dealing with a difficult person, give yourself a time limit or a limit of one insult and then calmly end the conversation.

Chapter 17
Establishing a Pattern

Recognizing behavioral patterns is an important skill that can help you predict someone's future actions. As Dr. Phil said, "The best predictor of future behavior is relevant past behavior." Establishing a pattern of behavior can take some time; however, if you observe and listen closely, the pattern will manifest right before your eyes. Patterns have a tendency to reveal themselves to those who pay attention.

Personality patterns are especially important in my line of business, as I need to figure out how my clients and candidates work, what makes them tick, what they like and don't like, how they like to communicate, how they make decisions, and so on. Some of my clients like to be wined and dined, while others prefer to communicate only by email and as little as possible. Knowing these personality patterns helps me to excel at my job and deliver effective results to both my clients and candidates. I have some clients I can send three résumés to and they will make a decision within a week about which of the three candidates they want to hire; I also have clients who want to interview thirty candidates and take months to make a decision. Knowing how each client operates and adjusting to their patterns is crucial to maintaining a productive relationship.

As a recruiter, I probe candidates for information about their professional behavior and ask open-ended questions. "Can you give me an example of a time when you were on a team and you made a mistake? How did you rectify the situation?" "Was your supervisor happy with the way you handled it?" I'm looking for an honest answer about how the candidate handled the situation: Did they act immediately? Did they accept responsibility for their mistake? Did the issue get resolved? What did they learn from the situation? There is no right or wrong answer. I don't want them to tell me what they think I want to hear — I want them to be honest, so I can get to know them and match them with the right job. Through these kinds of questions, I get to identify their patterns of behavior, which in turn helps me predict what type of role and company suits them. If a candidate jumps from job to job frequently, I will ask for the reasons for each move. "Why did you leave your last company after six months? Was it for money? Better job? Did you get fired? Did the company go bankrupt? What was your favorite job and why?" I continue to probe more and more to get a complete picture of the candidate's professional work history. This is not always easy, especially when candidates lie about why they left a company, or about a felony charge they got in college that they are hoping won't show up on a background check. Once I get to the point where I feel like I have enough information to work with, I begin the due diligence process of contacting their references.

Through personal and professional experience, I've learned to recognize the behavioral patterns of the individuals around me. Whether it's a girlfriend who is always late, a candidate who inflates their skillset, a boss who is a hothead, a friend who is insecure and in need of constant affirmation, or an ex-boyfriend who is a narcissistic sociopath, I am keenly aware of their behavior patterns and can predict how they'll react in a particular situation. Although these predictions are not 100 percent reliable every time, they're pretty darn close. Having an idea of how someone might behave under certain circumstances helps me figure out how I should handle the situation.

Sometimes I encounter a candidate who fudges certain details on their résumé by lying about having experience with a particular programming language or saying that they have a college degree when they didn't actually graduate or proclaiming to be a Harvard graduate when all they really took was a three-week summer course. In general, most candidates are truthful, but sometimes candidates lie when it's easier to tell the truth. Regardless, I take them at face value. I don't do a background check on every candidate I interview, only the candidates that my clients request before hiring them. It's really disappointing after several weeks of work to find out that a candidate's background check reveals a criminal record they never mentioned, or that there is no record of them ever earning a degree they claimed they had.

I had a candidate we will call Sam come into my office to meet with me and discuss his job options. Sam was twenty-eight years old, with a business degree from a top tier college. He was intelligent and handsome, with a personality oozing with charm. Sam told me he was recently let go from his former employer due to downsizing in the group. I pressed Sam for more details and began the probing process. I asked him a series of questions: How many people were in your group? Were any of the others in your department let go? Did you have a performance review? Was it positive? Were there any performance issues that you were aware of? His reply to all the questions was the same: "No, I had no idea I was going to get laid off; it was a complete surprise." "I was the go-to person in my group." "Everyone liked me." "The company didn't give me a reason when they let me go, they just said they were downsizing." Sam's story didn't seem unbelievable — in fact it was pretty common. I had no reason to doubt him, so I agreed to work with him and asked him for references, so I could verify his professional experience. He agreed and thanked me for meeting with him.

That afternoon, Sam emailed me the contact information for his references. Here is how the conversation with his first reference played out:

Me: "Hi, Gemma, my name is Poppi and I am the managing partner at The Z Firm. I am working with Sam and he listed you as a reference. Do you have a few minutes to answer some questions about him?"

Gemma: "Hi, Poppi, I can only verify Sam's employment dates. I am not permitted to say anything beyond that. It's company policy."

Some companies do indeed have such a policy in place, so, while it's frustrating for a recruiter, it's not unheard of to come up against this scenario when calling references. Still, I persisted:

Me: "I understand, but perhaps I can ask you some questions that you can simply say yes or no to?"

Gemma: "You can try, but I really can't give you any information other than Sam's employment dates."

Me: "Okay. Was Sam employed from May 2012 to November 2012?"

Gemma: "Yes, he was."

Me: "Was his position at the company an analyst position in the gas trading group?"

Gemma: "Yes."

Me: "You were Sam's direct supervisor, correct?"

Gemma: "Yes."

Me: "I can see from your LinkedIn profile that you are currently a gas trader at the company. Is that accurate?"

Gemma: "Yes."

Me: "Sam mentioned that he was laid off from the company due to downsizing. Is that accurate?"

Gemma: "I can't comment on that."

Me: "Is Sam eligible for rehire?"

Gemma: "No comment."

Me: "Did Sam have any performance issues?"

Gemma: "I can't answer that."

Me: "Is there anything else you can tell me about Sam that is important for me to know?"

Gemma: "No comment."

Me: "No problem, thank you for your time."

Reference number one didn't provide any information on Sam's performance. In fact, it made me more suspicious than anything else. I decided to do an off-the-record reference check with someone I knew who worked at the same company during the time Sam was employed.

Me: "Hi, Geoffrey, it's Poppi. Do you have a few minutes to chat?"

Geoffrey: "Hello, Poppi, what can I do for you?"

Me: "I want to ask you some off-the-record questions about a guy who worked at your company, Sam Haven."

Geoffrey: "Ah yes, Sam. Let me call you from my cellphone. I'm going to run downstairs for a smoke."

Ten minutes later…

Me: "Hi, Geoffrey, thanks for calling me back."

Geoffrey: "So what's up, what do you need to know?"

Me: "I'm trying to get a solid reference on Sam, but I can't seem to get anything of substance, only his dates of employment and his job title."

Geoffrey: "That's because he was fired for sexual harassment. Sam walked up to a girl on the trade floor, put an electric razor on her desk, and asked her if she would shave his balls. One of the senior managers happened to be standing nearby and reported him to HR. It turned into a pretty big deal, and the company launched an internal investigation."

Me: "Ah, so I guess he wasn't laid off like he said?"

Geoffrey: "No, the guy is a complete prick and an HR nightmare. He's kind of like that asshole in a motorboat that circles the other boats, making huge waves and pissing everyone off. It was only a matter of time. You should Google him, there's some good stuff out there."

Me: "That's all I needed to know. Thank you, Geoffrey."

Geoffrey: "You did not hear this from me."

Me: "Of course not, I Googled it. Thanks for the info."

After I hung up, I quickly Googled Sam Haven. An article popped up about an alcohol-fueled graffiti incident on his college campus, where Sam vandalized several buildings and monuments by spray-painting penises and balls on them. He was charged with criminal mischief and ordered to pay a fine of $20,000.

Now, it's not the penis-and-balls incident that really bothered me — those were just college shenanigans. Who hasn't done something stupid in college? It was the fact-finding mission I had to waste my time on when Sam could have told me up front. Had he revealed this from the beginning, it wouldn't have been a deal breaker for me.

When I know exactly what I am dealing with, that is when I am in the best position to help someone.

Sam had a pattern of inappropriate behavior, but he still had one lifeline left. I'm a believer in giving people second chances and the opportunity to redeem themselves, so that's exactly what I did. Sam had one strike thus far. Given his track record of inappropriate behavior, a public company most likely wouldn't touch him. However, there is a home for everybody, even people who have a lot of growing up to do. They're called private companies. They may or may not require the same background checks from employees, but they are a lot more likely to forgive a past transgression if the candidate meets all their other requirements.

I gave Sam one more chance, but his stories still weren't adding up. He continued to lie about the true reason he was no longer with the company, and I realized I couldn't trust him, so in the end I dumped him as a candidate.

When you're a good observer, you learn to recognize behavior patterns, you get better at identifying problems, and you find solutions faster; you can apply these pattern recognitions across all areas of human behavior. Police officers look for certain driving patterns for signs of intoxication, like weaving or driving too slow or too fast; psychiatrists look for signs of psychopathy through behavior patterns like the examples on Hare's psychopathy checklist: glib and superficial charm, grandiosity, pathological lying, etc.; airport security staff look for odd behavior patterns to identify potential terrorists; customs agents look for suspicious behavior to identify drug smugglers at border crossings. It is these types of patterns that are important and telling, so keep your eyes open, your antennas up, and soon you will notice the patterns yourself.

Key Points:

1. Recognizing patterns is an important skill that can help you predict someone's future behavior. As Dr. Phil said, "The best predictor of future behavior is relevant past behavior."

2. Recognizing a pattern of behavior can take some time; however, if you observe and listen closely, the pattern will manifest right before your eyes. Patterns have a tendency to reveal themselves to those who pay attention.

3. When you're a good observer and learn to recognize behavior patterns, you get better at identifying problems, which helps you find a solution faster.

4. Pattern recognition can be used across all areas of human behavior. Police officers use it to identify intoxicated drivers, customs agents look for odd behavior to identify drug smugglers, airport security staff look for suspicious behavior to spot terrorists, and so on.

5. Patterns are very telling and recognizing them is always a useful skill, so keep your eyes open, your antennas up, and soon you will notice the patterns yourself.

Chapter 18
Let It Go, Man, Let It Go...

Holding on to feelings of anger, jealousy, hurt, rejection, or failure will not allow you to move forward and develop. Learn to let go of negative feelings and you can conquer anything. It's that simple.

One night my husband, John, and I got into an argument on our way to dinner with some friends. It was about 7 p.m. when I arrived home from work and John told me we had dinner reservations at 8 p.m. at Tony's, a fine-dining restaurant on the outskirts of downtown Houston. I had no idea we had dinner plans, so I began to panic when John told me I had twenty minutes to find a dress, freshen up my hair and makeup, and head out the door. I'm not sure if he forgot to tell me about the dinner or if he told me and I forgot, but in any case, I was quite flustered. John had gotten home from work an hour before me, so by the time I got home he was already dressed and relaxing on the couch with a glass of bourbon. At 7:15 John came into the bathroom and said, "We need to leave in five minutes. Are you almost ready?" A bit frustrated, I replied, "Yes, I know, John, I'm going as quick as I can." John said nothing. He just stood in the doorway watching me curl my hair while he sipped his bourbon. I became irritated that he was hovering by the door, so in a sharp tone I said, "You standing there isn't helping me go any faster. I'm going as fast as I can." John walked away, and a few minutes later he went out to start the car. Time was of the essence, so I decided to finish my makeup in the car. I zipped up my dress, threw on a pair of stilettoes, grabbed my purse, and rushed out the door. John had been patiently waiting for about ten minutes when I swung open the car door, jumped in the passenger seat, and said, "Let's go!"

John backed out of the driveway and headed toward the restaurant. I asked him to please drive carefully and not slam on the brakes, so I could finish my makeup. At the first stop sign, John thought it would be funny to do a brake check while I was putting on mascara. He slightly tapped the brakes, just enough that I flew forward, and my mascara wand hit the top of my eyebrow. I was so irritated and turned to glare at John. "Really?" He chuckled slightly and said, "Sorry, I didn't mean to do that," though I knew he did it on purpose.

John picked up speed when we came to the entrance ramp of the freeway. I knew this was going to be bumpy, so I briefly stopped putting on my makeup. John began speeding up to merge with the oncoming traffic; my body pushed back to the seat as if I were on a roller coaster. John quickly moved across three lanes of traffic to the far-left lane and adjusted his speed from 90 mph to 65 mph. I resumed putting my makeup on; I was almost finished anyway. John quickly changed lanes to the right to pass a slower car in front of us and then moved back to the left lane. He did this a couple of times before he saw a police officer behind him and his fear instinct kicked in. Worried the police officer was going to pull him over for speeding, John quickly slammed on the brakes to slow down. He looked worried as he checked in the rearview mirror to see if the police officer was going to turn his lights on.

Trying to apply makeup was turning out to be a real challenge. When the police officer was no longer in sight, John resumed his normal driving pattern of weaving in and out of traffic. I was beginning to feel sick to my stomach from so much movement, so I closed the vanity mirror, put the visor up, and put the makeup away; I stared out the window, so I could see the road and calm my motion sickness. John seemed to be in his own world, listening to the radio and changing lanes like it was an obstacle course; that was standard driving procedure for him. He was tailgating the cars in front of us and then swiftly changing lanes in front of other cars at the last second. These were all maneuvers that left him very little room for error. After several more lane changes, I yelled at John to slow down. There was no need to drive that aggressively. John scoffed. "I know what I'm doing, Poppi, just sit there and relax." Telling me to relax is one of my pet peeves and probably the most irritating comment John could have made. Not only did I not relax, I did the opposite. I came unglued and started lecturing him about his lousy driving and how much it scared me. Being in a car with someone who drives like a NASCAR driver is not my idea of fun. I prefer *Driving Miss Daisy,* where at least I will feel safe and less nauseous.

John and I bickered for the entire ride, until we pulled up to the restaurant. I was so irritated I could barely even look at him. But once we arrived, I stopped arguing, took a deep breath, and said, "Okay, that's all I have to say about your driving. Now let's go have a good rest of the night." My tone was very matter-of-fact but I made myself clear. I knew I had to change my attitude and let go of the anger I had toward John, so I made the decision to get over it. No matter how mad I was, I could put the anger aside and not let it ruin my evening.

John and I walked into Tony's to find our friends. As luck would have it, they were running late. We went ahead to our table and ordered some hors d'oeuvres. We pretended the argument had never happened. This was very difficult for me, because I wanted to finish yelling at him. However, I controlled my tongue. When the anger welled up, I redirected my thoughts to something positive, like what I was going to eat for dinner. I realized I was starving, and then I remembered the HALT acronym: hungry, angry, lonely, tired. Before reacting, I asked myself if I was hungry, angry, lonely, or tired, and that was my reminder not to let the situation get out of hand, because I wasn't thinking clearly. I was determined not to allow my mind to go to that negative, angry place, so I simply *let it go*. After about fifteen minutes and a glass of red wine, the anger was beginning to subside.

Our friends finally arrived thirty minutes late and very apologetic. They had to make a stop to get gas and ended up in horrible traffic. Both of them seemed frazzled and appeared to barely be speaking to each other. John and I completely understood — we had had the same issue ourselves. I chuckled and repeated my mantra in my head: "Let it go, man, let it go…" Our friends, however, didn't seem to be transitioning so well and took sarcastic digs at each other for most of the night.

Learning to let go is much harder than it seems; however, once you get the process down, you will open your mind to positive growth.

In my professional life, learning to let go is a must. If I held on to the feeling of frustration every time a candidate lied on their résumé or a client changed direction and decided to put a role on hold after I'd been working on it for months, I would not get anything done. Instead, I've learned to change my perspective and revise my thinking. I allow myself to *feel* the frustration, but then I let it go.

Of course, how easy it is to let something go depends on the situation. Sometimes the circumstances are more serious and have more dire consequences than others. For example, if your partner is having an affair or a friend betrays your trust, it's not as easy to simply *let it go.* However, even in those cases eventually you still have to learn how to move on, or the negative feelings will eat you up from the inside.

Key Points:

1. Learning to let go requires you to change your perspective and revise your thinking. You can allow yourself to feel the disappointment, but then you *let it go.*

2. Before reacting, remember the HALT acronym and ask yourself if you are hungry, angry, lonely, or tired. If the answer is yes, try to delay your reaction until you are in a better state of mind and thinking more clearly. Otherwise, the situation might get out of hand.

3. Holding on to anger, jealousy, hurt, rejection, or failure will not allow you to move forward and develop.

4. Learning to let go of negative feelings is healthy, liberating, and the key to keeping your sanity.

5. Don't let negative energy weigh you down. Know what's important enough to go to war over, but let the small stuff go.

Chapter 19
Communication... Oh, the Many Ways

Learning how to be an effective communicator comes with practice. It all starts with self-awareness: You have to know what you want to express before you can figure out the best way to get the message across. So, you need to have clarity and self-confidence, and then you need to work on the most appropriate delivery for your message in order for it to have the desired effect. To be a good communicator you also need to stand your ground and remain in control of your emotions, which is why it's important not to let negative thoughts and feelings cloud your judgment.

If you go through life holding on to feelings of shame, low self-worth, anger, or fear, you are holding yourself back. Releasing these feelings is a cleansing act and it will help realign your values, rebuild your belief system, create a fresh starting point, and, most importantly, increase your odds of reaching a favorable outcome in any confrontation.

There are several ways to communicate negative and positive feelings in a forum that works for you. In the following paragraphs, we will explore those ways and provide solutions to help you communicate in a clear and skillful way.

Have you ever said to yourself, *I'm going to laugh about this someday?* During a crisis or a stressful situation, having a sense of humor is one of the most powerful tools of all. Humor coupled with positive thoughts can be used as a coping mechanism in any scenario. If you can step back and find even an ounce of humor in whatever is happening, it helps you to regain perspective and not allow yourself to become overwhelmed by anger, insecurity, grief, worry, regret, or fear. Even the most dire circumstances often have an element of the ridiculous about them. If you can identify that, you will be able to adjust your frame of mind, and then you can move forward toward solutions.

Another strategy to reframing a difficult situation is to actively choose to focus on the positive. Try to find the silver lining, no matter how thin it might appear. If you can hold on to even the smallest trace of optimism, you automatically change your state of mind and begin to soften the sting of bad news and frustration.

Pollyanna, a bestselling novel by Eleanor H. Porter, is a classic children's book published in 1913. It's about a little girl who was orphaned and sent to live with her rich but cold aunt Polly in a small New England town called Beldingsville. Pollyanna's unique outlook on life is about seeing the sunny side of any situation, no matter how grim it might appear to be. She was put to the test one Christmas when she was desperately hoping to get a doll from the missionary barrel and ended up with a pair of crutches instead. Rather than wallow in disappointment, she began playing "The Glad Game," a game her father taught her which involves finding something to be glad about in every situation. Instead of being upset about not getting the doll she so badly wanted, she became glad that she didn't have to use the crutches that she got instead. Pollyanna's optimistic attitude carries over to the Beldingsville community when she teaches some of the disheartened townspeople how to play "The Glad Game" and revolutionize their outlook on life for the better.

Pollyanna is put to the test once again when she is hit by a car and loses the ability to use her legs. Lying in bed grief-stricken, she is unable to find anything to be glad about and her positive outlook on life darkens. The townspeople begin telling Pollyanna stories of how she changed the lives of so many people by finding something to be glad about no matter how difficult the situation was. Little by little Pollyanna recovers from the grief and learns to be glad that she at least had legs that worked at one time. Eventually Pollyanna begins to walk again and learns to appreciate walking and not being disabled.

To illustrate Pollyanna's optimistic philosophy in practice, there is no better scenario than having a frustrating travel experience. John and I were flying from Houston to New York for a weekend getaway when we were faced with a few setbacks. Due to the cold, rainy conditions in New York, our flight was going to be delayed by an hour. Although it was an inconvenience, it was only an hour, which was no big deal. John and I sat in the black faux-leather chairs by the check-in booth right outside the terminal and watched the screen display the updated flight information. I flipped through a *People* magazine while John played Angry Birds on his phone; we were for the most part content. An hour later, the screen changed: Our flight was going to be delayed by another forty-five minutes. The ticket agent also came on the microphone to announce the flight would be delayed, because safety was their number-one priority. John and I looked at each other and sighed. We had to wait another forty-five minutes, but we understood. I went back to flipping through my magazine while John pecked away on his phone. We were a bit frustrated but there was nothing to be done.

Finally, the ticket agent announced that they were ready to begin the boarding process. John and I quickly jumped out of our seats, grabbed our carry-on bags, and headed for the front of the line; we were ready to get on the plane and relax.

As we boarded the plane, I turned to John and said, "What do you want to bet that we'll sit next to a crying baby?" John raised an eyebrow and said, "Stop jinxing us." I chuckled. "I'm just saying…"

We located our seats, stuffed our luggage in the overhead bin, and settled in for the three and a half-hour plane ride. John sat in the coveted window seat, claiming his shoulders were too broad to sit in the middle, which is what he always does. I gave him a look of contempt as I wedged myself into the middle seat. We played this game every time we traveled. There was no point arguing. We sat watching passengers impatiently scramble to find their seats; the mood of the plane was irritable.

I turned to John:

Me: "Let's play 'The Glad Game.'"

John: "I'm glad you always volunteer to sit in the middle seat."

Me: "I'm glad you think it's voluntary."

John: "I'm glad you always give good advice."

Me: "I'm glad you know I am never wrong."

John: "I'm glad you have all great ideas."

Me: "I'm glad you make me laugh."

John: "I'm gladder that you actually laugh at me."

Me: "I'm glad that you have big muscles."

John: "I'm glad you have big smile."

Me: "I'm glad you like my bossy personality."

John: "I'm glad you are a strong woman!"

Me: "I'm glad you think I am a strong woman."

John: "I'm glad you tolerate me when I'm sour."
Me: "I'm glad you don't smell sour."
John: "I shower twice a day."
Me: "I'm glad you are smart."
John: "I'm glad that you are smart and driven."
Me: "I'm so glad you said that."
John: "You win 'The Glad Game.'"
Me: "I'm glad you don't want to play anymore."
John: "Whew!"

Although the dialogue was ridiculously silly, John and I couldn't stop laughing. The normal mix of serotonin and dopamine in our brains had clearly reached an all-time high, because silliness and laughter were flowing over like a bottle of freshly popped champagne. We might have been laughing from the pure high of exhaustion, but "The Glad Game" worked, and, before we knew it, we were taking off.

Using humor to manage stressful situations is a powerful tool that helps to alleviate negative emotions or conflict. Humor lightens the mood, reduces stress, and prevents a conflict from escalating. By choosing to laugh rather than get mad, you change your perspective and the situation becomes less overwhelming, and therefore easier to cope with. Whether your car breaks down on your way to a job interview or you accidentally shave your eyebrows off, the benefits of finding humor in everyday life cannot be overstated, especially when the alternative is to have a mental breakdown. If you see that the situation is about to implode, reframe it immediately by finding the humor or the silver lining. At that very moment, you are making a conscious choice not to go down a negative path, which means you are already on your way to finding a solution for whatever problem you're faced with.

One last note on humor: The intent of humor should be positive. If your reaction is to take a dig at or make fun of someone, you are using sarcasm or mockery, not humor. In my experience, whenever I have crossed paths with someone who is constantly sarcastic, I've found that their intent is a putdown, not lighthearted humor. Sometimes the insult is followed by a comment intended to smooth it over, such as, "I'm just kidding." These can be backhanded compliments like "You're really pretty, for a fat girl," or passive-aggressive comments like "You are terrible at your job — I'm just kidding." There is a big difference between humor and sarcasm, and the tone of the situation will vary according to which one is used. Make an active effort to find the humor in challenging circumstances, have a laugh, and turn that frown upside down. Sometimes, a little bit of humor is exactly what you need to keep it together.

How do you react when you get angry? Do you yell or name-call? Throw things? Shut down? Cry? Do you say hateful things you later regret? My answer to the above questions is yes; I've done all of these. However, through experience and practice, I now respond in a more productive way that yields a healthier outcome. It's important to know yourself and your triggers. Once you know how you are likely to react, you begin paying more attention to your feelings, and it becomes easier to stop yourself from spiraling out of control.

I had a marriage counselor tell me once that when my ex-husband and I got into an argument, we should each go into separate rooms and write down our feelings. He told us to write down anything we wanted to say to each other, what had made us mad, and how exactly we felt at that very moment. So, I tried it. I went into a quiet room (my closet) and wrote down 300–400 things I didn't like about him (that I could come up with so many should've been a warning in itself, perhaps, but that's another story): He was rude, dishonest, belligerent, insensitive, irritating, condescending, belittling, mean, selfish, stupid, etc. After about fifteen minutes, I felt better. Ridiculously better. A jillion (is that a word?) times better. Although this method can be time-consuming and requires control, it works. Another strategy I've tried with John when we are disagreeing is to tell a joke every two or three minutes. It's funny and it helps to break the tension, but it's not necessarily appropriate for serious arguments.

Me: "Why did you purposely undermine me in front of the children?"

John: "I didn't, you did it to yourself."

Me: "Did what, asked you not to feed them Harry Potter jelly beans for breakfast?"

John: "They are Harry Potter Bertie Bott's Every Flavor Jelly Beans, to be exact. You brought the candy into the house. They were crying, it was easier."

Me: "So it's my fault you gave the kids whatever kind of jelly beans for breakfast, after you said you wouldn't, because I brought them into the house and it was just easier?"

John: "It's been two minutes."

Me: "Seriously? Fine. How do you make a tissue dance?"

John: "How?"

Me: "You put a little boogie in it."

John (laughing): "That's pretty good. I've never heard that one before."

The conversation went on for a little longer; however, after two more minutes and another bad joke, we were both laughing, and the argument no longer seemed worthwhile. The point is, we defused the situation with humor and did not allow it to get any worse. The argument wasn't important enough to get wrapped up with.

Another option is to talk to a trusted source, someone you are comfortable with — a friend, therapist, priest, parent, or even a stranger if you so choose. It can be liberating to talk to someone who doesn't know you, because you won't worry that they will judge you or that they have a vested interest in the situation. Sometimes you just need to get something off your chest and vent for a bit. You can also write your feelings down in as much detail as you want. By writing your story down, you are freeing yourself from the emotions by processing them, and you're allowing your mind to settle so you can move beyond the event. Either way, the process has a cathartic effect and is another tool to keep in your mental rolodex.

What is the best way for you to communicate when you are angry? Find out what works best for you. There are several ways to get your feelings out, both figuratively and literally. And by out, I mean out of your mind and out of your system, so you can restore your mental and emotional balance and allow yourself to grow. Writing down your feelings is a great tool that quickly changes a negative mental state to a more manageable one. You create a more useful thought process to make better decisions and remain in control over your actions. You can also write a letter to the person you are angry with, keep a journal, go for a run, throw some gloves on and have your way with a punching bag, or any other outlet that helps you release the negative feelings and gives you some perspective.

Another valuable reminder for when you're faced with a challenge is to stay focused on positive self-talk rather than putting yourself down. Instead of saying, "The entire work project is a disaster," tell yourself, "This project is massively annoying, but I will get it figured out." You might even inject some humor into the mix, because things can always be worse. The bottom line is that these mental exercises will help you respond with less anger and manage your emotions, so they don't get the best of you.

I will end this chapter with a story about giving a verbal card to someone. A verbal card is a way of giving a birthday card, thank you card, or any kind of greeting card without giving the person a physical object. Instead, you verbally tell the person what you would have written in a card, and you usually make it up on the fly. This is not necessarily appropriate in arguments and tense situations — it works better when you have something positive to say. There are many benefits to verbal cards, including making the person beam with excitement, instantly lifting their self-esteem, and creating a flurry of positive emotions. People's reactions might surprise you. The only downside is you can't go back and read the card later or put money in it, but you can still sing.

I saw someone give a verbal card one night at a birthday party for a friend of mine, Mike Morrison. His wife, Natalie Cochran, owner of Disegno Studio in Houston Texas, was sitting at a table with a friend of hers. At one point her friend leaned in and put her hands out to hold Natalie's hands and told her she wanted to give her a verbal card. I watched Natalie put her hands in her friend's hands, and then her friend began telling Natalie how much she appreciated her as a friend, respected her work as an artist, thought she was a beautiful person, and loved her kind nature. Natalie's face instantly looked struck with emotion and her eyes began to get red and watery. It was quite moving to watch Natalie's expression as her friend continued telling her in detail how much she loved and respected Natalie as a person, and how meaningful their friendship was to her. Not only was it emotional for Natalie, it was emotional for everyone at the table to witness.

Sometimes, just hearing something that somebody else likes about you can make all the difference in how you feel about yourself and the other person. When John and I were dating, I would randomly ask him to name three things he liked about me. The question put him on the spot every time, but his responses always filled me with joy and self-confidence. Here's one exchange I remember:

Me: "Honey, what do you like about me?"

John: "Everything."

Me: "Seriously, what are three things you like about me?"

John: "What do like about me, Poppi?"

Me: "Well… I love your dry sense of humor, your logical mind, you are fun and adventurous to travel with, you are comfortable in who you are, I find you extremely attractive, you're principled in your career, parenting, and personal relationships, and I believe you. Your turn."

John: "Umm, let's see. You're beautiful and I find your confidence sexy, you are passionate about your career, you're intelligent, focused, and you have a great sense of humor. When you laugh, I can see so much energy burst from your smile, and I love your dedication to me and your children. But, more importantly… you have great jugs."

Me: "Wow! I didn't expect you to belt out something with so much substance. You really think I have great jugs?"

John: "Works for me."

Me: "There's your verbal card!"

Although I hadn't intended on making the conversation into a verbal card, the exchange simply turned into one. I was fighting back tears, but they were happy tears. Inside, I was bursting with happiness from the things John said he liked about me. It made me feel really special to hear him say them out loud. I was not only surprised by some of his comments, I was completely taken aback. I had no idea John saw those qualities in me, and knowing he felt this way about me made me feel exceptional. I had no idea it could be that simple, but by naming a few things we liked about each other, both of us ended up beaming with pride. As our relationship evolved, I would randomly ask John the same question and then intently listen for his new and improved reasons of what he liked about me. Be careful though — use the question sparingly, as you can quickly wear it out.

Key Points:

1. Humor is a powerful tool that can defuse a conflict. By choosing to laugh, you change your perspectives and the situation becomes less overwhelming and therefore easier to cope with.

2. Make sure to distinguish between humor and sarcasm; humor is lighthearted, and sarcasm is mean.

3. Along with using humor, you can also put a positive spin on a challenging situation by playing silly games like "The Glad Game."

4. A verbal card is a way of giving a greeting card to someone without giving them a physical card. Instead, you verbally tell the person what you would have written in a card and you usually make it up on the fly.

5. Remember, sometimes hearing the way someone feels about you can make all the difference in how you feel about yourself.

Chapter 20
Don't Get Hooked

Have you ever been in a discussion with someone who wound you up and said something that got under your skin? How did you handle yourself? Did you lose sight of the true topic of the conversation and become emotionally focused on that one cutting comment? This is called taking the bait, and it's a habit I personally have the most trouble with. I not only repeatedly fall for this trick, I know when I'm falling for it and I still do it. I've come a long way though, and now I recognize this cheap tactic when someone uses it against me and I have more control over my reactions. Don't get hooked.

For some people there is no greater pleasure than goading you into a conversation where they are looking to sting you with their words and then sit back and watch you lose your cool. My ex-husband was a master of this tactic and still is to this day. I don't want to give him any props because he is just an antagonist at heart; however, he gets the first-place ribbon for this one.

One night, John and I went out for dinner while the kids spent their usual Wednesday evening at their dad's house (per the divorce decree, my ex gets the children every Wednesday and every other weekend). John and I had a great time chatting up a storm and winding down from a long day at work. After dinner, we decided to go home and take a quick dip in the pool before the kids came home. As soon as we got home, I headed for the bathroom to put on my bathing suit and grab a robe. I went out to the backyard to wait for John and sat down on the side of the pool and dangled my feet in the water. The water was a bit cold for me, so I kept testing it inch by inch with my feet until I was up to my calves.

John walked out to the front of the house to check the mailbox, which I could not see from the pool, but I did see a pair of headlights beaming against the garage door. I assumed it was my ex dropping off the children and I didn't think much of it; however, soon I could hear two male voices that sounded like they were yelling. I waited for a few minutes to see if I could make out what they were saying but all I could hear was a heated conversation. I pulled my feet out of the water and walked to the front of the house to see my ex face to face with John. I ran out the front door and shouted, "What's going on?" My ex was trying to start a fight with John and was goading him to push him or hit him. John calmly looked at my ex and said, "Don't walk up to me like that. You need to leave my property." My ex leaned forward in a threatening manner but eventually got back in his truck. He was showboating in front of the children and trying to get John to take a swing at him, but John didn't bite. He recognized exactly what my ex was trying to do and simply insisted that he leave. My ex gave it his best shot to try and goad John by calling him names and aggressively standing in front of him, but John didn't take the bait.

Unfortunately, triggered by many past interactions, I did take the bait and rushed to get between the two of them and then proceeded to yell at my ex that he needed to get his fat ass back in his car and leave. I'm sure I said some more colorful things while ushering the children into the house, but at that very moment I got a quick glimpse at my ex and he had the most satisfied smile on his face. He had gotten me to react in anger, yell at the top of my lungs, and call him awful names in front of the children. The children had a look of surprise and fear on their faces while they watched grown adults act like five-year-olds throwing a temper tantrum.

The drama was unfolding just as my ex wanted it to, and I knew at that very moment that I had fallen right into his trap. The children huddled together, unsure what to make of the situation. It was disheartening to know that my ex was getting so much pleasure by causing the children and me so much pain. One look at their helpless, alarmed faces and I knew I had to get them into the house as soon as possible.

After my ex left, John and I walked back into the house to calm down and have a talk with the kids about what had just unfolded. I was so mad at myself for losing my temper in front of the children and calling their dad names that are forbidden in our house, but it happened and there was nothing I could do to take it back. The way I handled the situation was wrong. I had no control, no grace, and no integrity in the way I reacted.

John, on the other hand, handled the situation with tremendous grace. He did not lash out in anger, he did not yell, and, more importantly, he did not take the bait. While my ex was baiting John by calling him names and puffing up his chest as if he was going to beat him up, John remained calm and asked him to leave. No yelling, no antagonizing, and no falling into his trap. That is, until 1 came into the picture and gave my ex exactly what he was looking for — a screaming match. Although my hysterical response came from fear and surprise, I should have had more control over my reaction and responded differently. My children are going to remember me yelling and screaming at their dad, but they won't remember what exactly started the blowup to begin with. My ex was wrong in every way for sneaking up on John and confronting him in an aggressive manner, but that still doesn't justify what the children will remember from that exchange.

Afterwards, I asked myself: *What should I have done?* For some strange reason, the phrase "stop, drop, and roll" came to mind, only this was not fire safety training. It was more like "stop, think, direct," or STD. Who can't remember that?! STD can be used as a psychological tool to manage your emotions and reactions in a tense situation:

STOP: This is exactly what it sounds like. *Stop* what you are doing and take a step back, so you can process the situation. In my case, I needed to take a few seconds to figure out what was going on.

THINK: This is where a decision is made about how you should react. *Think* about what it is that you want to put into action. Are you going to fight or are you better off walking away? Yell or remain calm? In my scenario, I should have made the decision to not engage with an angry, irrational person in front of my children.

DIRECT: This is the part where an action takes place. You take the decision you settled on to *direct* and control the situation. In my case, I should have quickly directed the children into the house, told my ex-husband that we could talk some other time, and shut the door.

The idea behind STD is to condition your mind to respond in a proactive way and not a reactive way. It's a catchy phrase that is easy to remember and a helpful psychological tool to have at your disposal. It is important to note that STD is not a phrase — or a strategy — that will come naturally unless practiced over and over. Eventually, STD will be the first three letters that pop into your head when you find yourself in a difficult or uncomfortable situation.

You have the power to choose how you are going to communicate. By remaining in control of your emotions and not allowing someone to get you in a tizzy, you ensure that the situation is less likely to escalate. Don't allow anyone to wind you up so that you behave in a way that is beneath you, especially when you know that that's exactly what they are trying to do — goad you into acting in a way you will later regret.

Key Points:

1. Remember STD: stop, think, direct.

2. STOP: Stop what you are doing and take a step back, so you can process the situation.

3. THINK: Think about your action plan and decide what to do.

4. DIRECT: Take the decision you made, turn it into an action, and direct the situation like a boss. If you are in charge of your emotions, you will also be in charge of the situation.

5. STD is not a phrase or a strategy that will come naturally unless practiced over and over. Eventually, STD will be the first three letters that pop into your head when you find yourself in a difficult or uncomfortable situation.

Chapter 21
Defining Victory

How do you define victory? Is it winning at all cost, no matter what the stakes are? Is it winning every battle, no matter how big or small? Is your objective pride- and ego-driven only? Or is it only about winning the battles you know you can win? Picking your battles is a useful tool if you pick battles based on the likelihood of overall victory, but you must define what victory is to you. As Mandy Hale puts it, "You don't have to show up to every argument you're invited to."

No matter how much willpower and determination you have, sometimes the potential fallout is just not worth the fight or the win. Damaging your pride, having your morale plummet, being humiliated in front of others, and burning bridges can be much worse than losing a battle. Before you decide whether to engage or not, you have to assess if the situation is worth your time, energy, financial exposure, or potential damaged relationships. Arguing every point and fighting every battle are unsustainable in the long term, and all the petty victories become meaningless. Don't lose sight of the big picture.

A recent example I can draw from is a legal entanglement between Paige and Hades, who were introduced in Chapter 7. For six months, Paige and Hades had been in court over a legal issue regarding several months' worth of unpaid child support. They spent countless hours and a lot of money going back and forth through email exchanges and phone calls with their lawyers to try and come to an agreement, but to no avail. As a last resort, they tried mediation, which lasted for hours and cost thousands of dollars. They still couldn't come to an agreement or even close to one. Paige was frustrated to the highest level. There were not only the issues of unpaid child support and child support modification, but there was a third issue: Her teenage son wanted to live with his dad. It's normal for a teenage boy to want to live with his dad. Paige was requesting that her son attend weekly therapy sessions, so the transition from her house to his dad's house could be as smooth as possible, with a healthy outcome. Hades frowned upon therapy and felt it would be a waste of time; he believed their son didn't need it. Paige struggled to see why any father would deny his son the right to speak with a licensed therapist who could help resolve any issues and lead to their son's betterment. Still, she'd gotten nowhere, and she was left with no other choice but to force his hand in the matter through legal action.

It was one thirty in the afternoon and Paige was sitting in the courtroom next to her lawyer and her current husband, Brian, waiting for the judge to sit on the bench. The courtroom was so quiet and cold. Paige looked down at her hands and saw that her fingernails were purple, and she had goosebumps running up and down her arms. Hades was sitting on the other side with his wife and lawyer. Every little sound was amplified times ten, and anxiety was looming over everyone. Paige could hear the squeaking of the chair every time someone shuffled for a more comfortable position, along with small whispers coming from Hades and his lawyer, but she couldn't make out what they were saying. Paige's husband, Brian, looked catatonic, as if he were about to fall asleep waiting for the judge. She had no idea what to expect on this day; it was her first time ever testifying for anything.

Paige saw the bailiff quickly stand up as the judge came out of his chambers to approach the bench. The bailiff asked everyone to stand. The process seemed so formal. The first few minutes were a blur of legal jargon between the judge and the lawyers, of which she understood very little but tried to follow. Each lawyer made a brief opening statement directed to the judge as to the evidence that would prove each of their cases and support their demands. Hades and Paige had three children together. He was asking to pay $250 a month for the two children who would continue to live with Paige and asking her to pay him $1,700 a month for her son who wanted to live with Hades. This would be quite a significant change from the previous court order stipulating the current child support amount. Paige was struggling with the logic and math on this one. It didn't make sense to her, but she remained calm and took it all in. She told herself that no judge in his right mind would even entertain such nonsense. She kept looking at the judge's face to see if he was going to laugh at the numbers, but he didn't even look up from his computer screen. His face was blank, almost uninterested; Paige wasn't sure he was even paying attention.

After the lawyers presented their opening arguments, the judge had everyone stand and raise their hands to swear them in. *Here they go.* The first person called to the stand was Hades, because he was the petitioner. He stood up, adjusted his tie, and walked to the stand with arrogance permeating through his every move; it was obvious he felt confident. He took a seat on the stand and leaned back in his chair, as if he were about to watch a movie. Hades appeared to not have a worry in the world. His lawyer began asking him basic questions — his full name, the children's names and ages, etc. — and then she moved on to what I call layup questions. She asked him a series of questions about what kind of father he was, how involved he was in the kids' lives, why he lost his job, why he had been out of work for two years, why he was having such a difficult time finding a job, etc. He seemed to enjoy being the center of attention and breezed through the questioning with ease and a few chuckles here and there. An hour and a half went by; having to listen to so much self-promotion made Paige want to scream. He was the best at everything, blah blah blah.

Two hours later, finally, it was time for Paige's lawyer to cross-examine Hades. Paige sat up straight in her chair and gave him her full attention. Her lawyer's line of questioning was not as innocent as Hades' lawyers was. Now they were getting somewhere. Paige's lawyer began by asking a few basic questions and went over timelines, financial statements, number of job interviews, etc. She could see Hades beginning to look uncomfortable and squirming in his chair a little. He was claiming to spend hours each day applying for jobs; however, they had a record of only thirty-one emails from a two-year period. If you do the math, that means Hades sent out one and a half emails per month for the past two years. Pathetic. It's obvious he had not tried very hard to get a job, and he seemed to be enjoying cashing in his assets, which is how he was able to afford a couple of vacations, including one to Pebble Beach for a golfing tournament. Who knew being unemployed could be so much fun?

Paige's lawyer proceeded to ask more questions, digging a little deeper and deeper with each one. He asked Hades what his plan was for getting a job, and he replied that he used to be a bricklayer in his twenties, so that could be an option. Paige was gripping her hands so she didn't lose her composure - he was so full of crap. Who was going to hire a fifty-something-year-old bricklayer with back problems? That had "lawsuit" written all over it. Hades must have been getting desperate at this point, because he threw out that he was also considering getting his teaching license, and with that he would make $50,000 a year. Paige gripped her hands tighter, close to cutting off the circulation. Hades was trying to come up with a job that paid $50,000 a year, compared to the $300,000–$800,000 per year he had made for the last fifteen years working in corporate America, so the judge would lower his monthly child support to the minimum-wage amount. Hades said it was impossible for him to make that kind of money anymore, because the industry was stagnant, and nobody would hire him. At this point, he was beginning to show some strain and was babbling on and on about irrelevant details, like his best friend who was injured a year ago and his military father whom he hadn't spoken to in years. The judge was an ex-military lawyer, so he was trying to appeal to him any way he could, which is not a bad strategy, but complete crap. The judge showed no emotion or reaction.

Paige's lawyer continued asking questions regarding the six months of overdue child support. "Is there a reason why you decided to ignore the court-ordered child support judgment and not pay your child support when your bank account shows you had the money to pay it? In fact, your bank account shows you have a $40,000 available balance." Hades replied, "I was saving the $40,000 for the IRS. I didn't file my tax returns in 2012, so I'm on a payment plan where I pay $700 a month." Paige's lawyer looked down at his notes for a few seconds and then asked,

"If you are on a monthly payment plan, then why is it necessary to keep $40,000 in your bank account and not pay your child support?" Hades' expression was blank. "I don't know, I just did."

"No more questions, Your Honor"

Now it was Paige's turn to testify. She was nervous and shaking like a leaf, but she kept reminding herself to just tell the truth, stick to the facts, don't talk too much, and everything would be fine. Her mantra was playing over and over in her head: "Don't be afraid, be brave," and she was owning every word of it. Her biggest worry was Hades' lawyer trying to get her confused and exasperated so she would lose her composure on the stand. Paige's lawyer told her it was a common trick used by other lawyers, so she focused hard on not going down that path. She was committed to remaining calm, answering Hades' lawyer's questions with dignity, and being respectful, no matter what she threw at her.

Paige was on the stand for a total of thirty minutes which didn't seem like much compared to Hades testimony of an hour in a half.   Regardless, time felt like it went by really fast and she was relieved to have it over with. His lawyer's line of questioning was not half as aggressive as she expected it to be. She asked Paige questions about her career in Advertising and if she had ever tried to help Hades get a job, to which she replied, "No, I have not." She asked her if she thought of herself as successful, and what she thought of the relationship between Hades and her son who wanted to live with him, and a few more mundane questions. Paige expected her to try to paint her in a corner and then slam her with a series of questions that she didn't know the answers to, but she didn't. After she was finished, Paige's lawyer stood up to ask a few more questions about job seekers and what Paige think it takes to get a job in corporate America these days. Paige explained that in her opinion, Hades would need to be proactive and send out several resumes per week if he was serious about getting a job, and network heavily with his existing relationships. There were plenty of jobs available and as a professional in Advertising, Paige saw unemployed professionals get jobs in corporate America on a regular basis; even if they couldn't get the exact job they held previously, they could still get work. Inside, Paige was fired up thinking about Hades saying he was desperate to find a job, given that he'd sent out only thirty-one applications in a two-year period. That was wrong. So wrong. The crux of the matter was that Hades did not really want to get a job — he'd been enjoying not having to work, and now he needed to figure out a way not to pay child support. So, he'd decided to go with a change in his financial situation, claiming he is unable to get a job. He couldn't even get a minimum-wage job, according to him. Nobody would hire a fifty-something-year-old who has been out of work for almost two years. He insisted his only choice was to cash in his assets to cover his living expenses, which is excluded as income to the courts, even though he wasn't paying his child support. Bananas! Bananas! Bananas!

After five hours, the trial began to wrap up. It was 5:30 p.m., and traffic was going to be a nightmare. The judge explained that he needed to think about this case, so he would not have a ruling for until the end of the week. It was only Monday, so the end of the week felt like a lifetime away for Paige, but she could deal with it. She had no choice. Paige felt confident that if the judge was taking a whole week to decide, at least his judgment would be fair.

Brian and Paige talked about the trial the whole car ride home. Both of them felt good about the way the trial went. Paige thought her lawyer did a fantastic job and put on a solid case. She was glad to have the whole ordeal over with; They would have an answer one way or another by the end of the week.

Shortly after Paige got home, her phone dinged, notifying her she had a new email. It was from Hades. An email so soon after the trial? Paige was sure this would be good.

Paige,

You are a liar, and this isn't the only thing you lied about on that stand, and you know it. You're deplorable. To say our son and I have a difficult relationship is laughable. To say our son has an A in chemistry is a joke, he has never had an A in that class. You might learn how to use the school website.

And for the record he has NEVER been in an AP class. He was enrolled in K classes (advanced-placement classes), which he shouldn't have been. You could also benefit from some clarity on why these grades look like they do on this app (the school app where you can see your children's grades).

As far as your friend goes, you are a flat-out liar. (Hades had his facts mixed up and was insistent that Paige had submitted his résumé to one of her contacts, but that was incorrect.) You should be proud. Add to your résumé "proficient in lying before a judge."

Clearly, Hades wasn't feeling as confident as Brian and Paige were. His email was so bitter and nasty. They didn't even know the outcome yet, but Hades was already acting defensive. Perhaps it's not fun to get on the stand in a room full of people and admit that you haven't paid child support in months because you just didn't feel like it. So, Paige responded in kind.

Hades,

Why so bitter? You are mistaken. When I said our son had an A in Chemistry, I meant to say Geometry. Same goes for saying "AP" classes when I meant to say "K-Level" — they are both advanced classes either way. AP is what I called them growing up. It is easy to make a mistake like that when you are under pressure. However, a legitimate mix-up is not a lie as you so like to state. Perhaps your lawyer should have been a little more on the ball and asked me to clarify.

Regarding your resume, I was going to submit your résumé to a friend of mine that I do advertising for, however, because you had already contacted the company directly, they already had your resume. This was not made clear to me at the time I agreed to help you. I tried to clarify this at the trial, but your lawyer cut me off. Should I say you are a liar because you are mistaken?

Lastly, it is my opinion that the relationship you have with our son is difficult. Your lawyer shouldn't ask questions she doesn't want to know the answer to. Never works out well.

Having said that, I will not be adding "proficient in lying to a judge" on my résumé but I would suggest adding "bitter" to yours.

Paige

196

P.S. Please let me know if you come up with any other deplorable mistakes on my part, I don't want to disappoint you.

Paige

Paige,

You stated the wrong grades and classes. In your text message you said you had sent my resume to your friend, and that you told her my circumstances. That text was prior to me getting in touch with the company directly. Your timing is off. Either way, you stated differently on the stand.

If my relationship with our son is so difficult, why did he want to come live with me? You might want to think about that some more.

Hades

Hades,

So, I've thought about my comment that your relationship with our son is difficult and I stand by it. Like it or not, it's the way I see it and always have.

I was not wrong on the grades, I said he has two Fs, two Ds, one C, and an A, which is accurate. Band doesn't count.

I called my friend to ask her about the position BEFORE I sent her your resume, which is when I was informed that they already had your résumé on file. Again, I tried to clarify this on the stand, but your outstanding lawyer cut me off. Where did you find her, by the way? She was quite the legal eagle.

Paige

P.S. I was really impressed when you threw in your testimony about your military father and your best friend who had an accident, BUT you forgot to mention your dog who was hit by a car and your ingrown toenail that causes you to limp when you walk. A for effort on that one!

P.S.S. I think you should definitely consider being a bricklayer again, that was another really awesome idea. Bricklayers with back problems are in high demand.

Paige

Granted, responding sarcastically to his emails wasn't the most mature way for Paige to act, but it was the best unemotional response she had, given that he'd called her a liar. Paige hadn't lied, she'd kept her composure, and stuck to the facts. It was at that very moment that she realized just how much she had gotten to Hades. Paige was watching him become completely unraveled over an email and, of course, she was really enjoying it. Hades was already acting as if he had lost and was letting Paige know he did not like it. Seeing him get so mad and calling her names gave Paige GREAT satisfaction. It was her Charlie Sheen moment. Hashtag: #WINNING!

Friday evening came around and still there was no verdict. It'd been four days since the trial and the judge said he would have a ruling by the end of the week. Paige called her lawyer only to hear that there was nothing they could do but wait. It was the judge's domain. Even though she knew this, she continued to check the County Clerk website every few hours. Although the site wouldn't post the actual ruling, it would let her know if a judgment had been made, which would give her an idea of when she might expect to hear from her lawyer. Paige was keeping her impatience at bay by imagining that maybe she would be surprised, and a judgment would magically appear on the website. No such luck.

That weekend felt like it went by incredibly slow for Paige. By Monday morning, she was sure that there was going to be a verdict, but there was not. Paige was beginning to think the judge had forgotten about the case and needed to be conveniently reminded that they were still waiting to hear from him. Her lawyer did not think this was a good idea, so she waited.

By Tuesday morning, Paige was wildly frustrated. She kept wondering what was taking so long. She was tired of checking the website over and over, only to find no updates. To distract herself, she decided to Google the judge, and she found him on LinkedIn. There was nothing interesting on his profile — only his education and his current position as a judge in the Family District Court. For a brief second, Paige considered sending him a request to connect so he might remember her name and get on top of his ruling, but she thought better of it and shut the site down. Paige congratulated herself on the good choice she'd just made and mentally patted herself on the back.

Finally, on Tuesday evening Paige got a text message from her lawyer saying he'd just emailed her the ruling. His text didn't give her any indication about which way the judge ruled, so she rushed over to her computer to read the email. Paige was so nervous that she felt as if she was hyperventilating. She was prepared for a favorable judgment. Paige wanted to see Hades get hit with a ruling that served as a message to all the scumbags out there who don't pay their child support.

Instead, this is what was waiting in her inbox:

1.Father to pay 6 months of back child support – *DENIED*

2.Request that Father is intentionally underemployed – *DENIED*

3.Request for Father to follow dentist/orthodontia recommendations – *DENIED*

3.Father is to pay standard minimum wage monthly child support of $250.00 - GRANTED

4.Mother is to pay monthly child support of $1,700.00 - GRANTED

5.Mother is to pay Father's legal fees of $5,500.00 - GRANTED

6.Request for Father to pay Mother's legal fees - *DENIED*

7.Psychological session for son - GRANTED

Paige was stunned. She couldn't believe what she was reading. Paige kept thinking there must be a mistake. Not only was the judge not making Hades pay for months of overdue child support, he was making him pay only $250 a month for two children and requiring Paige to pay Hades $1,700 a month for her son who would be living with him. AND she was required to pay Hades' legal fees. The ruling was simply unbelievable. Paige still couldn't breathe normally. She was emotionally shell-shocked. Why would a judge rule this way? Had Paige made him mad? Had she failed to help him in the past too? Why would he reward Hades, who was purposely trying not to work so he didn't have to pay child support, and allow him to get away with this? Why would he rule so heavily and unreasonably in his favor? It made no sense to Paige at all. The judge's ruling was egregious, unethical, and discriminatory. To say Paige was astounded would be an understatement. She was mentally knocked out. She trusted that the legal system would be fair, but it wasn't. Not only was she completely disheartened by the ridiculous ruling, she no longer had any trust in the legal system. Paige kept telling herself to breathe. Good air in, bad air out. Breathe in, breathe out. How could this happen this way? How was she supposed to fight judicial corruption?

After Paige sulked for a few hours, she decided to come to terms with the situation. Hades had won the legal battle — so be it. Now it was time to move on and let the bitterness go. The only positive outcome of the ruling was that Judge Asshat (the kindest name she could think of) had granted psychological services for her son while he went through the living transition. There was a silver lining in the ruling after all, and at least it was for the betterment of their son. Unfortunately, Judge Asshat did not find Hades to be deliberately underemployed and granted him the minimum-wage child support standard, taking him from $2,700 a month to $250 a month and making Paige pay Hades $1,700 a month. Ouch.

Hades' strategy worked: he lied, he pleaded poverty, and he won. Paige was so angry — unbelievable angry. She felt wronged and betrayed by both Judge Asshat and Hades. So, she decided to vent her feelings on paper. Paige sat down on her bed and began writing how she felt about Judge Asshat's ruling and how unfair the situation was. She furiously wrote every hateful feeling she was currently experiencing. It was doubtful that she would even have enough paper to put down all the thoughts she wanted to get out of her system, but she continued writing away until she began to feel less angry. Paige included her feelings for

Hades as well as her disappointment and frustration with the corrupt Judge Asshat.

After a while, once Paige started to get a grip on her emotions, she decided to try to make the best of the situation, since she had no way of changing it. There had to be a lesson somewhere in this unfairness. Paige asked herself what she had learned from this experience. Little by little the lessons came to her: 1. Never assume you know how a judge is going to rule. 2. The legal system is a sham. 3. Sometimes you just don't win; sometimes people lie; sometimes people are corrupt; sometimes life isn't fair, so toughen up, buttercup.

After Paige finished her venting session, she decided to go online and read reviews of Judge Asshat. They were eye-opening. He had a reputation for being corrupt and prejudiced against women, and for ruling favorably for fathers with military backgrounds and for lawyers who donated money to his campaign dinners. Hades did not have a military background, but his father did, and Hades had made a point to mention that on the stand at great length. Once again, Paige was stunned by the injustice. After reading these reviews, she was no longer surprised that he ruled against her. It seemed inevitable. She wondered if her lawyer knew about the judge's reputation, and if so, why he never warned her.

Review 1: "Judge Asshat is corrupt and prejudiced against women and does not do what is in the best interest of the child. The judge ruled to give my ex-husband custody of our 6-year-old little girl. She doesn't want to live with her dad and step mom because she feels they don't care about her. This year I will petition the court unfortunately I will be seeing Judge Asshat again. He is not for the best interest of the child. He is for father's rights period."

Review 2: "Judge Asshat is a horribly unfair biased judge who sides with military fathers and does not believe that mothers have any rights. He rules for the law firms and lawyers that are in the Houston clique and have contributed to his campaign dinners. You will not win in his court if you are going against one of his favorite and influential law firms. I haven't seen my daughter in 9 months. He allows my husband to legally kidnap my child."

Review 3: "Judge Asshat seems to come across as a fair and just judge. The truth is he is as corrupt as they come. 'Best interest of the child' is an idea he does not subscribe to. If you have money you can buy your verdict in the court with the 'Honorable' Judge Asshat."

Review 4: "I was in front of Judge Asshat and went at it alone because I was denied counsel by this judge. I am not an unfit mother and never dreamed of the day this judge would let a father who never wanted anything to do with his child for seven years get custody. I was floored when this judge tore my child from me and her brother for no reason. Yea, my ex was military, and I think that played a big role in things. I thought one had to be the worst parent in the world to have this happen. My fight is not over and will appeal this bad judge and his ruling."

Review 5: "How do we get rid of this dishonest judge? Let's keep Asshat out of the courts."

Review 6: "Judge Asshat presided at my daughter's child custody case which lasted almost 2 years. Overall his case seemed prejudiced toward the military staff for reasons not to go into detail, however I'd use caution when selecting him as the judge if you have one spouse that is military; especially the male side."

The bad reviews went on and on. It was clear that Paige could never have gotten a fair trial with a judge so biased toward the military and biased against women. His mind was made up before she even stepped foot in the courtroom. At least she now had an explanation as to why he ruled the way he did, but that didn't make the situation any better.

Paige's options were limited at this point, and she needed to figure out how to proceed. She could appeal the ruling, which would cost upward of $100,000, according to her lawyer. But the appeal would automatically circle back to Judge Asshat's court, which he would deny, so there was no point in going down that path. What were her chances of winning the appeal and getting the judgment overturned? Did it financially make sense to go through the appeal process? The answer was no. It would be a financial disaster, and her chances of getting the ruling overturned were slim to none. This was a battle Paige was going to choose not to pursue. Her solution was to redefine what victory meant to her. The victory was getting her son therapy. As far as the rest was concerned, Paige accepted the outcome of the trial and moved on. Or at least she would move on after she wrote a concession letter to Hades. Yes, she did that.

Hades,

As you are aware, the ruling from Judge Asshat came in last night and he conspicuously ruled in your favor. Let there be no doubt, while I strongly disagree with his decision, I accept it. Judge Asshat appears to come across as a fair and just judge, but his appearance is deceptive. He is known for ruling in favor of his favorite Houston law firms and lawyers who contribute to his campaign and he did just that (Hades' lawyer was an Asshat campaign contributor). Judge Asshat had the power to wound and he did. He will have to answer for that someday. Having said that, I accept the finality of the outcome and I accept my responsibility, which I will deliver unconditionally.

Paige

The concession letter was more for Paige than for Hades. She wanted him to know that she did not agree with the outcome but that she accepted it and would honor it. Even though Judge Asshat and Hades did not show her the same courtesy, she would rise above the disappointment and keep moving upward and onward. Nobody gets the best of Paige, not anymore. Hades never responded to the email.

Defining what victory means to you is a tool that helps you examine the importance of a situation and the likelihood of a positive outcome. If you're facing a losing battle to begin with or if it results in the destruction of relationships, personal well-being, financial security, etc., then maybe you take a step back and don't engage. Even if the odds are in your favor, you are not guaranteed a win. However, with this tool, you give yourself peace of mind to know there is a victory in every outcome somewhere — you just have to find it and let the rest go.

Key Points:

1. Defining victory is a tool for making decisions based on the likelihood of victory and the risk of destruction of your personal well-being, financial security, or relationships.

2. Define what victory means to you — is it to win at all costs or is it to choose wisely based on the probability and the cost (financial and otherwise) of a win?

3. Even if the odds are in your favor, that does not guarantee a victory. Be prepared for the possibility that you will lose.

4. Examine the importance of the situation, define your victory, and then accept the results unconditionally. Don't get bitter, get better.

5. There is a victory in every situation, you just have to find it.

Chapter 22
Toughen Up, Buttercup, and Use Your Anger Wisely

Have you ever been fired from a job? Betrayed by a colleague you thought was a friend? Passed up for a promotion? Did you get angry? Excellent! You are on your way to making a big change. Anger has its place in personal and professional relationships and, if harnessed properly, can have great benefits. It's an incredibly powerful emotion that provides us with insight into ourselves. Sometimes this is exactly what you need to act courageously, move forward, and become more resilient. Don't suppress your anger — leverage it.

Being emotionally resilient and mentally tough are important tools that help you recover from a difficult situation, manage the unexpected, and take your failures in stride. At some point in life, you will face adversity — for example, an unexpected death, a divorce, a lawsuit, an unfaithful partner, a robbery, a failing grade, etc. It's the courage to shake it off and move past the adversity that builds mental fortitude and resilience, and it's how you evolve as a person.

Have you ever said or done something you regret? Did you replay the scene over and over in your mind until the pit of your stomach was aching? Good news — you're not alone.

Rich Kinder, a well-respected business tycoon, is a great example of the power that anger can play in growth. Kinder, the former president of the energy giant Enron

Corporation, was in line to be the next CEO at Enron. In 1992, Kinder and the CEO at the time, Ken Lay, had agreed to a succession plan where Kinder would become the next CEO within five years and be in control of the day-to-day operations. However, in 1996 the Enron board of directors engaged Lay for another five years as the CEO, passing up Kinder. Kinder was so angry at this betrayal that he resigned from his position shortly thereafter.

After resigning from Enron, Kinder partnered up with Bill Morgan, and they started their own pipeline company, which is known today as Kinder Morgan. Kinder and Morgan built an extraordinary business that became one of the largest, most respected energy companies in North America (the United States and Canada), worth billions of dollars. Shortly after Kinder's departure, Enron imploded, and several top executives were sent to prison for fraud.

Enron was formed by Ken Lay in 1985 in Houston. In 2001 Enron filed for bankruptcy due to fraudulent accounting practices. Ken Lay (CEO), Jeffrey Skilling (CEO and chairman), Andrew Fastow (CFO), and other top executives had misled Enron's board of directors, auditors, and employees by hiding billions of dollars in debt from failed business dealings, all the while encouraging people to buy Enron stock to drive the price up.

The top Enron executives were indicted, and most served prison time. Ken Lay was found guilty of ten counts of securities fraud and died of a heart attack three months before he was to be sentenced. Jeffrey Skilling was convicted of federal felony charges and is currently serving a twenty-four-year sentence. Andrew Fastow was found guilty on multiple counts of fraud and served six years in prison. Enron became known as the largest corporate bankruptcy in America.

Just like it happened for Rich Kinder, some of your greatest accomplishments will come from being betrayed and getting pissed off. He quit out of anger, not just because it was the right thing to do and went on to become one of the most successful businessmen in the energy industry. By getting angry and leaving Enron, he also narrowly avoided getting wrapped up in one of the largest corporate scandals in American history. It goes to show you that sometimes an event that causes you great anger and disappointment at first may turn out to be a blessing in the long run.

It's the anger that causes you to rethink your behavior, decide to make a change, and act. If your anger is used intelligently, it can be a positive tool that promotes personal and professional growth. It's normal to feel angry when you are in a situation that is unjust or threatening; however, out-of-control anger can be damaging to your career, personal relationships, and overall mental health. But, within reason, anger is an excellent motivator. Use it wisely.

Have you ever heard anyone say they were so angry they couldn't think straight? It's true — your mind becomes laser-focused on the anger and temporarily freezes your coping skills, therefore rendering you less efficient. Be aware of that risk and try not to give in to your emotions to the point where you lose control.

My brain short-circuited one night over a stupid flippant comment I made to a client, thinking I was being funny. I was not. It was the Christmas season, and, as is typical for Houston this time of year, it was hot and muggy outside, close to eighty degrees. Bright Christmas lights and colorful decorations lined the streets. My client, whom I will refer to as Sterling, wanted to meet after work to go over a candidate he was interested in hiring through my firm. We agreed to meet at an Italian restaurant that was on his way home from work, so he could pick up a piece of Italian wedding cake to surprise his wife with. When I arrived, I saw Sterling from across the room. He is 6'5" and usually wears a cowboy hat and has a cigar hanging out of mouth, so he is not hard to spot. He sat at a table in the bar drinking red wine with two other people. The place was swarming with bigshot professionals, so I assumed that's who the people with Sterling were, based on their corporate attire. The restaurant was packed with hungry customers crowding around the bar area, waiting to be called when their tables were ready. The wait staff moved from table to table as if they were a busy colony of ants; the vibe in the restaurant was intense and the patrons seemed to be having a jolly good time.

As I maneuvered around the crowd, Sterling saw me and turned to wave me over to the table. He then introduced me to the other two people. "Poppi, this is Ron, our controller, and Evelyn, our compliance officer. These two keep me in line." Everyone chuckled. I shook hands with both of them and took the last open seat at the table. Although I was expecting to meet only Sterling, I was thrilled to have the opportunity to also meet some of his employees in a social setting, which is great for business development.

Sterling has always been one of my favorite clients to do business with. Maybe it's because he reminds me of my dad, or because he is hospitable, well mannered, and charming. As a client, Sterling has always been laid back, easy to deal with, and a straightforward communicator. He knew what he was looking for in a candidate and he made hiring decisions quickly, which is a recruiter's dream; we like deals that close fast.

The four of us sat around the table making small talk for a few minutes, until Sterling turned his attention to me and said, "So, let's talk about this candidate you have. Is she interested in our company and what is it going to take to get her to make a move?" Perfect, that's exactly what I wanted to talk about. We had a fifteen-minute conversation about the candidate, then the waiter brought a to-go bag with the piece of cake Sterling had ordered for his wife. He apologized for having to leave so soon, but he said he had some Christmas errands to take care of. Sterling encouraged us to stick around and enjoy the wine, shook our hands, and left. I stayed behind to pick up the check, which is normal protocol when trying to win business from a client. I ended up talking with Ron and Evelyn about how long they had been at the company, how many kids they each had, what they had planned for the holidays, and so on. Everything was going so well, until…

My phone rang, and it was Sterling. I walked away from the table to answer it, in case he had something to say that his colleagues weren't meant to hear. "Hi, Sterling, did you change your mind and decide to come back and join us?" He laughed. "No, I'm on my way to play Santa Claus but had a quick question." I chuckled. "Are you going to ask me to sit on your lap?" There was a moment of silence, then Sterling responded, "Pffff, I am on a speakerphone with my wife heading to a play. I was calling to ask if we had a recruiting contract in place with your firm." I froze. A sharp pain shot through my stomach, and the entire room felt as if it was spinning. His response was not what I expected. Somehow, I found my voice and said, "Oh my God, I was just kidding. Yes, we already have a contract in place, so that won't be a problem." "That's all I needed, thank you," Sterling responded curtly and hung up the phone. I was completely stunned. What was I thinking? How could I say such a stupid thing?

I walked back to the table with a blank look on my face. Although Evelyn and Ron hadn't heard a word of the conversation, I was in no mood to continue mingling. I said it was my pleasure to meet them, put down some cash, and darted out of the restaurant. The next part is a big blur. I was so stunned that I couldn't function. I was extremely embarrassed that I had said something so stupid not only to him but to his wife. The worst part was that there was nothing I could do to fix the situation.

My stupid attempt at being funny had backfired big time. I worried about the conversation the entire evening, replaying the events over and over in my head. "Stupid, stupid, stupid. Why, why, why did I say that?" I was sure I had lost the account, but it was the mindless comment and humiliation that bothered me the most. That kind of joke was completely meant to be funny — it's just something that came out of my mouth before my brain had time to catch up with the words. That evening when I went to bed, I tossed and turned most of the night. I was so preoccupied that I was barely able to close my eyes.

I woke up at 5 a.m. feeling as though I'd been hit by a bus. My eyes were red above dark puffy circles. You could see that I hadn't gotten much sleep — the stress was written all over my face. I reached for my phone and began scanning through my emails. My breath caught when I saw one from Sterling. The subject line read "Trade Floor Talk" was addressed not only to me — he had also copied the other two partners at his company and the VP of Human Resources. My stomach began to hurt again, my ears began to ring, and I could feel my chest tightening. I opened the email, not knowing what to expect, and read through it line by line. It was a painful email to read, but it was something I needed to hear. I had messed up big time, and the email said just that.

Sterling had written a reproachful message about my off-color comment. He went on to say that he had been married for twenty-five years and his wife doesn't need to hear "trade floor" banter. Although my comment would have been funny in some other setting, it was not ok at that moment. Yep, I know that now and will never forget!

I could feel my mouth dry up as I read his words, and my heart was beating so fast it felt like it would jump out of my chest. I didn't know I was on a speakerphone with his wife listening. I was embarrassed and riddled with regret.

After reading and rereading his email several times, I began feeling that his response was overly harsh and a gross overreaction to my comment. Normally, Sterling wouldn't have skipped a beat with an off-color comment, however this time was different, his wife was on the other end of the call and the comment didn't translate well. Even though I felt that way, I mustered up the courage to reply. I had tried to be funny and I'd failed. It was imperative that I acknowledged his comments in the email and apologized for my horrible choice of words. I vowed I would not do or say anything inappropriate again, and I apologized to his wife and to the other partners in the company as well.

Over the next few weeks, I continued to quietly wage war with myself. I replayed the phone conversation and the harsh email over and over in my mind. I had not heard anything back from Sterling after I sent my apology email, and I was unclear on what to do or where we stood. Did he want to still do business with me? Should I call him? Should I send something to his office? What was the appropriate action to take? I had heard nothing about the account, and I was ridden with anxiety. I needed to find a way to come to terms with what I had done. It was time for me to get up, dust myself off, and get back in the game. So, that is exactly what I did.

Step one was to own my behavior and acknowledge that the situation was 100 percent my fault. I typed a letter to myself, making sure to include every detail from the conversation. Step two was to write down my feelings, thoughts, and fears that stemmed from the incident. This was the easy part — I was filled with so much regret that it came pouring out. Every horrible feeling I had about myself, and every consequence I feared — I wrote them all down: embarrassment, shame, and regret about being so improper; feeling like an idiot; possibly losing a client, and so on. Did I say "embarrassment" yet? I was sincerely devastated. However, the more I wrote down my feelings, the better I began to feel, and the shame subsided. It was as if the negative feelings were slowly melting away with every word I wrote. Step three was to come to terms with my behavior, forgive myself, and move on. I owned my poor choice of words, apologized, and vowed never to make that mistake again. That one mistake was not going to define me from here on out. It was over, lesson learned.

In the end, I did not lose Sterling as a client, and I still have a good relationship with him and the other partners to this day. It's true that the relationship is not the same as before, but I am okay with that. I was able to bounce back, forgive myself, and move on.

Everyone is going to make a mistake at some point. It's inevitable. When that happens, acknowledge your own actions and take responsibility for them. Pay attention to the painful feeling in your gut, the sweat beading on your forehead, and the tightening of your body. Know that these physical reactions are your mind's way of alerting you that there is a problem to be dealt with. You will probably be angry at yourself for making a mistake, the way I was about the comment to Sterling, but instead of beating yourself up endlessly, channel the anger into making sure you learn your lesson and never repeat the same mistake again. Toughen up, buttercup, and leverage your anger wisely. You are about to evolve to a greater level of self-awareness and, most importantly, resilience.

To end this chapter, I bring you Johnny Cash's number-one hit "A Boy Named Sue," which has a lot to do with mental toughness and resilience. The song is about a boy whose dad named him Sue before he left him and his mom when Sue was only three. Growing up as a boy named Sue was tough. He got picked on and made fun of a lot, and he got into many fights. So, Sue vowed to kill the guy who named him Sue, if he ever ran into him, which he does one day. He's ready to fight his dad, but then his dad tells him he named him Sue because he knew it would make Sue tough and help him survive without his father in the world. Sue ends up making up with his dad once he understands why he was named Sue. So, I ask you — what if you were a boy named Sue? How tough would you be? Would you learn to survive anything that life threw your way?

Key Points:

1. Resilience is the ability to bounce back from a difficult situation and keep going. When you get knocked down, shake off your failures and try again.

2. Humor is a tool that helps you to stay resilient when facing a challenge.

3. When you make a mistake, pay attention to the painful feeling in your gut, the sweat beading on your forehead, and the tightening of your body. Know that these physical reactions are your mind's way of alerting you that there is a problem to be dealt with.

4. Anger is an incredibly powerful emotion that can provide us with insight into ourselves. If your anger is used wisely, it can be a positive tool and a powerful motivator that promotes personal or professional growth.

5. Don't suppress your anger — leverage it.

Chapter 23
Role Models and Mentors

Whom do you admire? Whom do you aspire to be like, act like, look like? What is it that you admire so much about that person? Whom do you credit for your personal or professional success? Was this person a role model or a mentor? Role models are people you look up to and perhaps aspire to be like. Mentors are people who care about you and take an active part in shaping you either personally or professionally.

Growing up, I was an aspiring gymnast with a fantasy of being in the Olympics. Although I started gymnastics at age nine, which is way too old to begin training for a sport if you want to be in the Olympics, it still didn't stop me from tumbling, cartwheeling, and leaping all over the living room. When my mom took me to the grocery store with her, the aisles became tumbling runways for me. When she took me shopping with her at Macys, I would practice handstands in the dressing room while she tried on clothes. If we were in a parking lot, I would balance my way across the parking blocks as if they were beams, and if we were standing in line, I would flip around the steel barriers until I was told to stop so I wouldn't break my neck. One time I even twirled into a shelf full of jelly at the grocery store; I was trying to imitate Mikhail Baryshnikov in a scene from *White Nights* where he says, "Eleven pirouettes, eleven rubles." I pirouetted right into the glass jars, which came flying down all around me, smashing into hundreds of pieces all over the floor. One jar even hit me in the head, and I got cuts on my legs from all the glass. The world was my gymnastics stage, and I couldn't help myself from leaping, spinning, and flipping all over it. Being yelled at by my mom in front of the grocery store manager while covered in jelly wasn't fun, though it was worth it.

So, where did my inspiration come from? The one and only Mary Lou Retton, the dynamic gymnast who won, in the 1984 Summer Olympics, a gold medal in the all-around, two silver medals, and a bronze. Her floor routine was packed with power and personality, and she dominated the event with a radiant, fierce determination. I wanted to be just like her. Mary Lou was on the cover of every major magazine, including *Newsweek, Sports Illustrated,* and *Time*, to name a few. She scored two perfect tens and was on the Wheaties box with her energetic smile and confident champion pose. Her floor routine was so powerful that she received a standing ovation from the crowd — she was on fire. Mary Lou was my role model.

Role models are important for everyone — doctors, lawyers, students, children, men, women, teenagers — everyone. We need someone to look up to and model our behavior after. Mary Lou did those things for me. I would practice my floor routine for hours in the front yard, tumbling from one corner to the next, imagining myself performing in front a roaring crowd cheering me on. Mary Lou's energy and confidence resonated with me. I was truly inspired every time I watched her perform. And, like every tween in the eighties, I cut my hair in a shaggy bowl cut just like Mary Lou's. Although, to be fair, it did not look as good on me — my hair is curly, so on me it looked more like a Bozo fright wig.

Unfortunately, I was not good enough to be the next Mary Lou, but I did get to train with her coach, Bela Karolyi, for a summer program, and that was good enough for me. I wasn't ready for the dedication and commitment it took to be a Mary Lou, even though she made it look so easy. The hours and hours of practice and the diet restrictions ruled me out pretty quickly. Boys and a social life took precedence once I hit my teens.

As I got older, my role models changed. I admired movie stars with strong characters who overcame great adversity, like Will Smith in *The Pursuit of Happyness* or Tommy Lee Jones and Robert Duvall in *Lonesome Dove,* where their word was their bond. These characters inspired me to be an upstanding person, to try hard, to push myself even when I wanted to quit, and to not feel sorry for myself. They had it much harder than me and still managed to accomplish so much. If they could make it, I knew I could make it.

As of today, the most inspiring movie character to me, hands down, is Donnie Yen in *Ip Man* (or *YIP Man* — the spelling varies). Yes, I like kung fu movies. I binge-watched *Ip Man* 1, 2, and 3 in one day and felt empowered to overcome anything that crossed my path. The movie is loosely based on Grand Master Wing Chun, teacher of Bruce Lee in the 1930s in Foshan, China. After a Japanese invasion, Ip Man loses his wealth and is forced to work in a coal mine to support his family. The conditions are brutal, food is sparse, and the workers are treated like slaves. When Ip Man's friend Li Zhao is unjustly killed, he becomes enraged and challenges ten men to a match at once and impressively defeats them all. The story goes on about Ip Man's struggles to protect his friends and family, leaving him with no other choice but to fight. Eventually, he defects from the mine with his family to Hong Kong, where he opens a school to teach others the art of Wing Chun (a Chinese defensive martial art).

What is it that inspired me so much about *Ip Man*? The words that come to mind are depth, ethics, values, harmony, virtue, dignity, and moral responsibility. The way he approached life was so simple: "We all have inner demons to fight, we call these demons, fear, hatred and anger. If you do not conquer them then a life of one hundred years is a tragedy. If you do, then a life of a single day can be a triumph."

In my professional and personal life, I am often in a position of leadership. To think of what it means to be a strong leader, I think of Ip Man and the way he rallied an entire town to band together and stand up for themselves. The townsmen respected him, trusted him, followed him with confidence, and wanted to see him succeed. I think about his approach to humility and emotional intelligence when dealing with my clients, candidates, employees, and my own children. When I struggle with work-life balance, I defer to Ip Man's philosophy on values and know that it is equally important for me to be a wife and a mother as it is to be a boss and a friend. I also reflect on and try to follow Ip Man's code of conduct, which is displayed at martial art schools all over the world.

Ip Man's Code of Conduct

1. Remain disciplined

2. Practice courtesy and righteousness

3. Love your fellow students or classmates

4. Limit your desires and pursuit of bodily pleasures

5. Train diligently and make it a habit

6. Learn to develop spiritual tranquility

7. Participate in society — be conservative, cultured, and gentle in your manners

8. Help the weak and the very young

9. Pass on the tradition

People can be shaped not just by role models but also by mentors — perhaps it is a combination of both or a plethora of all the above. Different people see different aspects of us that influence our careers and personal lives, and their perspective can help us to deal with challenges as they arise. I have had professional mentors who encouraged me to use my voice and speak up; another solidified the importance of finishing what I start, no matter how big or small the task; there are other gymnasts who inspired me to want to be the next Mary Lou Retton. Mentors encourage and inspire us to develop areas within ourselves that we don't necessarily see. They give us advice, ideas, and options as to how to accomplish what we are seeking to do. Having a mentor is a tool that provides a roadmap — it helps us navigate our path and shape our inner selves.

I have had several personal and professional mentors: first of all my dad, Frank Lytle, who instilled a strong work ethic in me and made sure I understood the importance of follow-through; my gymnastics coaches of many years,

Patty Newman and Patty Chizmar, who pushed me to power through setbacks and remain focused under pressure; my mother, Paula Draper, who taught me the uplifting power of retail therapy, a.k.a. shopping, and always making sure my outfits were well put together, no matter the occasion; my stepmother, Darlene Lytle, who was unequivocally dependable and fiercely supportive of me and my family; my English teacher in high school, Mr. Karanga, who showed me compassion and taught me not to judge others; my first boss in the energy business, Mr. Glover, who took an interest in developing my career and showed me the qualities of a strong leader and how important it is to pay attention to detail; my mother-in-law, Carolynn Kevlin, for being the voice of reason and a strong sounding board; and my husband, John Wartes, who taught me how to let go of anger and to love again. Find people you admire and trust, people who take a personal interest in your well-being, and then soak up what they have to teach you. Those lessons will help shape your future self.

Everyone needs somebody to believe in and someone to believe in them. Embrace the benefits of having a positive role model or mentor and be proactive about finding one. If you don't have role models already present among your family and friends, think about celebrities you admire and try to follow their example. As far as mentors, those are often teachers or more senior people in your chosen line of work. Figure out whom you want to be like, and then try to get them to teach you and help you along the way as you learn and grow. Sharpen your observation skills, focus on a behavior you want to emulate, and engage with them as much as possible. I assure you, these life-changing souls are everywhere.

Key Points:

1. Role models are people you look up to and perhaps aspire to be like. Mentors are people who care about you and take an active part in shaping you either personally or professionally.

2. Role models are important for everyone, no matter their age, gender, or professions. We all need someone to look up to, to model our behavior after, and to inspire us to do better.

3. Find someone you admire and trust, someone who takes a personal interest in your well-being, and soak up what they have to teach you. Those lessons will help shape your future self.

4. Having a mentor is a tool that provides a roadmap — it helps us navigate our path and shape our inner selves.

5. Remember Ip Man and his inspiring rules: "We all have inner demons to fight, we call these demons, fear and hatred and anger. If you do not conquer them then a life of one hundred years is a tragedy. If you do, then a life of a single day can be a triumph."

Chapter 24
Tell Your Story

One of the reasons I decided to write this book is because I had something to share about my life experiences. Everyone has a story, and everyone has something to express, so why not pass on your wisdom to others? Hearing others' stories, experiences, ideas, and words of wisdom can be just what someone needs to connect the dots and make a positive change in their life. There are many different platforms to share your story: Talk to a friend, talk to a stranger, write a book or a blog, write a screenplay, make a movie, speak at a seminar, write an anonymous letter, be a guest speaker, give a TED talk, be a counselor; these are only a few of the many possibilities.

It's about finding the platform that works for you and that will allow you to reach the people who can most benefit from what you have to say. Your stories are unique, and by sharing them you offer inspiration and can help others to learn about various subjects and to overcome obstacles in many different aspects of life, from religion to violence to politics to losing a loved one to addiction to legal issues, and many more. We all benefit from each other's experience and wisdom, and if you are willing to share your failures and triumphs, then you have the power to make a difference for someone else and to change the world for the better. Telling your story not only gives you a voice, it gives others the courage to find their own voice. Do it.

My friend Helen Sharkey is a great example of someone who took adversity by the horns and turned it into a powerful message to help others. In 1996, Helen worked at Dynegy, an energy trading company located in Houston. She was thrilled to accept a position as an accountant and described it as her dream job. Helen worked on the team that created Project Alpha, a project designed to take complex transactions that usually included derivatives and collateralized debt instruments (as, for example, a group of banks doing one loan). Helen was one of the lower-level accountants assigned to the project when she found herself in the middle of an investigation by the Securities and Exchange Commission. The project was found out to be a multimillion-dollar scheme to inflate the company's cash flows, and because Helen did what she was told, and signed her name on certain documents, she had unknowingly become an accomplice. "Did I feel in my gut it was wrong? Absolutely. Did I think it was illegal? No way," she said. Helen didn't want to challenge the hierarchy and make waves, so she just went along with what she was told to do, even though it didn't sit right with her. Little did Helen know that she would become a scapegoat.

When she was twenty-eight, Helen and two other senior-level management employees were charged with conspiracy to commit securities fraud, and she was sentenced to thirty days in prison and a $10,000 fine. Shortly after giving birth to twin boys, Helen served her thirty-day sentence in a maximum-security federal prison. After her release, she put the incident behind her and focused on raising her boys and trying to get back to her life. Helen did go on to have a normal, fulfilling life. She also had a new message for aspiring CPAs just entering the corporate world. She wanted to share her experience in order to help others avoid her mistakes.

I had the pleasure of working with Helen in 2007 and heard her story firsthand. She was very candid about her experience and I found her experience to be both scary and fascinating. What happened to her could easily happen to any one of us, so we can all learn from her message.

Helen now speaks regularly at seminars, luncheons, and college campuses on topics of compliance, accountability, and ethics, to serve as a warning to accounting professionals of what you should do if you are in a situation like the one she was in and how to recuse yourself from what you think might be wrongdoing. She talks about what life was like in prison, about how an act of kindness gave her the strength to go on, about some of the lessons she learned, such as trusting your gut and looking out for yourself, and about learning that there is always a light at the end of the tunnel. Helen faced her adversity with dignity and had the bravery to tell her story to others who could learn from her experience. We need more people like Helen in the world, people who are willing to expose themselves and their own mistakes and embarrassments so the rest of us can avoid going down the same path.

Another example of personal courage is Caitlyn Jenner, formerly known as Bruce Jenner, who is a well-known openly transgender woman, winner of the 1976 Olympics decathlon in Montreal and also a reality TV personality on *Keeping Up with the Kardashians* and *I am Cait.* She speaks about finding the power to overcome adversity and about the personal struggles she went through to transform from a man to a woman. In 2015, Jenner came out publicly as a trans woman, changing her name to Caitlyn and completing sex reassignment surgery in 2017. Caitlyn received massive media attention over her transformation, including both praise and a large amount of backlash from individuals who did not see her behavior as courageous and who insulted and attacked her relentlessly. Despite the animosity, Caitlyn bravely and openly spoke about her lifelong struggles with gender identity for all the world to hear and take courage from. She. Told. Her. Story.

In 2015, in front of a national audience, Caitlyn walked across the stage in a long white Versace gown at the ESPYS in Los Angeles and accepted the Arthur Ashe Courage Award, a sports-oriented award given to top athletes or people who have revolutionized sports. She gave a ten-minute speech about the difficulties of her transition and championed the transgender community, receiving a standing ovation. Although Caitlyn delivered a phenomenal speech, she received fierce backlash from her critics; many thought she was not a deserving recipient of the coveted award; some may have questioned her contribution to sports, but many others were simply admitting to their transphobia. Caitlyn's critics felt there were more worthy candidates, like Lauren Hill (now deceased), a nineteen-year-old freshman basketball player at Mount St. Joseph University who courageously battled cancer while continuing to play basketball in her final days and encouraging others to make the most of every day. Way to go, Lauren, and way to go, Caitlyn. Both of you are courageous and worthy candidates.

I end this chapter with a challenge to you: Tell your own story. Look at it as something you simply must do, no matter how big or small your story may be — find a platform and share your experience. Forget about being judged; just focus on your message and let it flow. Maybe you have a rags-to-riches story, a story about an addiction, or about surviving abuse, about quitting a job you hated, a funny story about the time you walked out of the bathroom with toilet paper hanging out of your pants, or an empowering story of triumph where you won the decathlon.

Whatever your message might be, remember that stories are the most powerful human connector. Sharing our experience is how we relate to each other. Regardless of your station in life, if you are rich or poor, successful or not, with a small or big audience, it's still worthwhile to try. Someone out there will be thankful for your story. They await your words.

Key Points:

1. Telling your story is a powerful tool that cleanses your mind and educates and empowers others.

2. Choose a platform that works best for you and your story: Talk to a friend, talk to a stranger, write a book or a blog, write a screenplay, make a movie, speak at a seminar, write an anonymous letter, be a guest speaker, give a TED talk, be a counselor — the list goes on.

3. Your life experiences matter and your stories are unique. Tell others what you have learned, what you would do differently next time, what you would do the same, and share the advice you believe to be important.

4. If you are willing to share your failures or triumphs, then you have the power to make a difference. Do it.

5. Be courageous.

Final Thoughts

As I write this book and remember my advice of simplified wisdom, I realize the difficulty of being my own advisor. I'm forced to analyze myself, hold myself responsible for solving my problems, and give myself the same tough love I give everyone else. This is hard to do, but I am taking my own advice, because it works. More importantly, I see the advantages that come from having a set of mental tools that effectively change my perspective and behavior for the better in challenging situations. As a result of using these tools, I am able to lower my anxiety, increase my happiness, self-awareness and insight, maintain a healthy perspective and an overall positive outlook on life.

I will share one last story with you, about pushing forward no matter what life throws in your path. Sometimes it doesn't matter if you're ready or not — you just have to keep rolling with the punches and make the best of the situation.

I was sitting in my Jeep in rush-hour traffic, on my way to a client meeting, when my stomach started rumbling and I began feeling queasy. Really queasy. The oysters I had eaten the night before weren't sitting so well, and I could feel it was about to wreak havoc on my system. A rash of goosebumps broke out on my arms and legs, and I knew I would need to find a bathroom, STAT!

I sped into the parking garage like an Indy 500 racer and parked in the first available visitor parking spot I could find. I quickly jumped out of my car, slammed the door, and walked fast, determined to find a bathroom, or maybe even just a dark corner at this point. I got to the front lobby, where I was greeted by a smiling security guard. I asked her where the bathrooms were. She told me I would need to sign in first, and then asked me what floor I would be going to. In a strained voice, I told her I was going to the ninth floor. She told me to go to the elevators behind her, go up to the ninth floor, go left down the hallway once I exit the elevator, and I should see a sign for the bathrooms. I scribbled my name on the sign-in sheet and dashed past her to the elevators. I pushed the up button and waited while several other people gathered to get on the elevator as well.

My situation had become even more urgent. Another wave of nausea and discomfort pulsed through my body, and I felt severely dehydrated and queasy. My muscle control was beginning to wane, and I was afraid that there wasn't much time left. I squeezed my muscles tight, very tight. I recited to myself: "Please, please, please, don't let this happen here."

The forty-five-second wait for the elevator doors to open felt like an eternity. I slipped in along with six other people and hit the button for the ninth floor. I'm pretty sure I pushed it 10 times, because everybody knows that makes the doors close faster. Staring straight ahead, I refused to make eye contact with anyone. I was trying not to draw attention to myself.

Finally, the elevator reached the ninth floor. The doors opened, and I slyly got off the elevator. I didn't bother to look back; I threw all my focus into fast-walking down the hallway looking for the bathroom sign. I had crippling nausea at this point and was doing the clenched-butt strut all the way down the hallway. I'm pretty sure this was helping my speed. I'd be lying if I said I wasn't panicking, but I kept telling myself, "You can make it, you can make it, you can make it." If there was ever a time I needed a mantra to keep my mind focused, this was it. Sweat was pouring down my forehead like Niagara Falls (no pun intended), and my head swiveled left, right, up, down, and all over the place as I desperately searched for the women's restroom. My digestive system could not have had worse timing. I was so glad I ate the oysters

Directly in front me, I saw my client's office at the end of the hallway, but no sign of a bathroom. I was at a breaking point, so I waddled even faster. I was pretty sure the undesirable was going to happen, and it was only a matter of seconds before a blowout occurred. I walked a bit farther and looked to my left. Finally! The women's restroom was right in front of me, just a few feet away. I sprinted toward the bathroom as if I were being chased by a vicious dog. I threw both hands onto the door and pushed it open with enough force to seriously injure anyone who happened to be behind it. I managed to fall into the bathroom, which was small, with only two stalls, but thankfully both were empty.

What occurred over the next five minutes can only be described as liquid hell. I thought I was going to die. I narrowly made it to the toilet and expelled the oysters from the night before with a vicious projectile-vomit, in a demonic way across the bathroom floor. WOW. Just WOW.

The nightmare felt as if it lasted an eternity, but the entire incident was only about ten minutes. I sat in shame. It was a messy situation, literally. I breathed a sigh of relief that I made it to the bathroom and didn't have to settle for the hallway. I shuffled over to the sink, which was small, maybe thirty-six inches wide. I feverishly pumped the stainless-steel soap dispenser mounted on the wall, draining the soap as I all but scrubbed my skin off. There was a good chance someone could walk in at any minute, so I was trying to get out of there as quickly as humanly possible.

After my improvised sponge bath, I dried myself off with paper towels that had the absorbency of notebook paper. I patted my face and neck down to wipe the sweat away and bolted out of the bathroom to go meet my client. It was time to get my game face on.

Before I walked into my client's office, I stopped for a minute to take a deep breath. I straightened my skirt, made sure my shirt was tucked in neatly, and said to myself, "Didn't see that one coming." I tried to take inventory of my situation and put it in perspective. Although it was pure misery, the situation could have been worse. I had a lot to be glad about. I felt lucky, grateful, and relieved at the same time. Lucky that I made it to the bathroom without leaving a trail of destruction, grateful that the night before I had gone to a seafood restaurant and not a chili festival, and relieved that no one had witnessed the McShitshow in the bathroom.

With the bathroom drama now behind me, it was time to focus on my client. I whispered a quick mantra to myself ("All good, lets go"), fixed an energetic smile on my face, swung open the door, and walked in cool as a cucumber. It was GO TIME!

My meeting went smoothly and lasted about an hour. Although I was worried about having another wave of nausea, thankfully I didn't have any more problems.

Life is going to happen whether you're prepared for it or not. Exactly when you least expect it, you will have a crisis, a moment you didn't plan for, or a situation you don't know how to deal with. For me, that moment came out of nowhere and quickly — like Usain Bolt breaking the world record for the 100-meter dash in 9.58 seconds. Thankfully my crisis happened in private and I made it to my meeting without anyone witnessing the raw oyster revenge. I wasn't prepared for a situation like that to happen; I didn't have a hazmat suit, cleaning supplies, an invisibility cloak, or a change of clothes readily available; all I had to work with were my mental tools. I powered through with grit, an empowering mantra, a sense of humor, courage, positive perspective, and fortitude. The stomach worries did not get the best of me that day. I used the tools, moved past the adversity, survived the ordeal, and shared my diarrhea-gate story with you. You. Are. Welcome!

Throughout my personal and professional battles with horrible bosses, crazy candidates, clients, ex's and disgruntled ex-employees, I've held onto one last piece of wisdom I want to share with you. Regardless of what anyone tells you or what you might believe about yourself at any point in time, don't underestimate yourself — or anyone else, for that matter. Everyone is capable of more than they think they are. Be a student of the mind, use the tools you have learned in this book, and know that you are now armed with the artillery you need to have a respectable outcome, no matter the situation. You have acquired a special set of skills (thank you, Liam Neeson from *Taken!*) to recognize and deal with manipulative people, let go of anger, grow through adversity, keep your wits about you, move forward, and leave behind a wealth of lessons for others.

I can't wait to hear your stories. Now, get out there and do something worth talking about! Even if it happens to be a case of the backdoor trots. IN PUBLIC.

CPSIA information can be obtained
at www.ICGtesting.com
Printed in the USA
BVHW070438181218
535790BV00014B/1441/P